SEASONS
AT THE FARM

ALSO BY
SHAYE ELLIOTT:

Family Table
Welcome to the Farm
From Scratch

SEASONS
AT THE FARM

YEAR-ROUND CELEBRATIONS
AT THE ELLIOTT HOMESTEAD

SHAYE ELLIOTT
Foreword by Stuart Elliott

GUILFORD, CONNECTICUT

An imprint of The Rowman & Littlefield Publishing Group, Inc.
4501 Forbes Blvd., Ste. 200
Lanham, MD 20706
www.rowman.com

Distributed by NATIONAL BOOK NETWORK

British Library Cataloguing in Publication Information Available

Library of Congress Cataloging-in-Publication Data

Names: Elliott, Shaye, author.
Title: Seasons at the farm : year-round celebrations at the Elliott homestead
  / Shaye Elliott ; foreword by Stuart Elliott.
Description: Guilford, Connecticut : Lyons Press, [2018] | Includes index.
Identifiers: LCCN 2018009935 (print) | LCCN 2018012311 (ebook) | ISBN
  9781493034727 (e-book) | ISBN 9781493034710 (hardback)
Subjects: LCSH: Agriculture—Popular works. | Country life—Popular works. | Cooking
  —Popular works. | Interior decoration—Popular works. | Handicraft—Popular works.
Classification: LCC S501.2 (ebook) | LCC S501.2 .E44 2018 (print) | DDC
  630—dc23
LC record available at https://lccn.loc.gov/2018009935

♾™ The paper used in this publication meets the minimum requirements of American National Standard for Information Sciences—Permanence of Paper for Printed Library Materials, ANSI/NISO Z39.48-1992.

Printed in the United States of America

For my husband, who has created a beautiful canvas for me to paint.
Thank you for your endless willingness to serve, even if that means
moving furniture again, and for giving me the most wonderful
reason to cultivate a beautiful home: love.

CONTENTS

The Joy of Summer 73

Autumn's Riches 141

Winter's Warmth 211

WINTER CELEBRATIONS 269

FOREWORD

by Stuart Elliott

It is good every so often (maybe more) to step back from the details of everyday life and attempt to get a big-picture view of things. As our eyes adjust to this high-altitude view, what comes into focus is a pattern. Like staring at a "Magic Eye" picture, the image that lies behind the pattern comes into focus. What is most evident from this vantage point is the cyclical nature of things. Like a wheel spinning in motion, life seems to revolve around something fixed, a permanent center, a hubcap if you will. This image-through-the-pattern seems to be a kind of force (not in a *Star Wars* kind of way) or a governing principle. Let's call it a Law of Life. As the wheel spins to make a complete revolution, what is also evident is that things aren't the same as before. There is both permanence (the wheel circles back to its original position) and change (things have happened in the time it took to spin). So, the wheel is not spinning in a vacuum; it has traction on the ground and each turn advances it down a path. Somewhere in all this constant motion our lives play out.

These are by no means novel or original observations. You have probably thought of them yourself and most likely in a way that makes more sense than I have. We hear something of this sentiment in the old adage people say when some event is about to happen: "History is doomed to repeat itself." The Byrds sang about it in the 1960s with the song "Turn, Turn, Turn." So did Journey in the 1970s with "Wheel in the Sky," though less poetically.

The Byrds' lyrics are adapted from an ancient Hebrew poem found in the book of Ecclesiastes. Unlike the sentiment we get from the Byrds' song, Qoheleth, the author of the poem, seems to be a little stressed about the Law of Life. He's been running around trying to figure out meaning and purpose, and all the while the Law of Life does what it does with or without him. "For everything there is a season, and a time for every matter under heaven," he observes. "That which is, already has been; that which is to be, already has been," he observes further. Qoheleth has come face to face with the Law of Life and it makes him cry out, in a kind of despair, a refrain he repeats throughout his writing: "There is nothing new under the sun" and "all of life is vanity, a chasing after the wind."

From our big-picture vantage point, if we were to observe the rate that has come to characterize life in our culture, I think we would see a frenetic pace that does not quite sync with the timing of the Law of Life. I think our growing restlessness as a culture and the quickened pace of our consumerist lives demonstrate, probably deep down in our hearts like Qoheleth, a battle with time.

The manner in which we sync our lives with the natural cycles of the Law of Life creates a kind of rhythm. And if you are at all like me, there are moments of stillness where the painful beauty of this law will impress itself upon you; you can almost hear the music playing behind it all, sometimes cacophonous, discordant, and dissonant, other times melodic, harmonic, and beautiful. Its beauty is like watching the bud of a rose develop and grow through its various stages to the climax of its elegant bloom. Its pain lies in knowing that, like the flower, it is not permanent, though we deeply desire it to be. I consider my own children growing and changing before my eyes. It brings me simultaneously great joy but also an almost inarticulate sorrow. I am inevitably drawn back in to consider the cyclical nature of the Law of Life. I once was where they are, though not precisely. They will be where I am, and the rhythm of this stretches back generations and will continue generations more.

The Law of Life, once perceived, is evident everywhere. But, for the homesteader and those more bound to the land, the rhythm of the law is most felt in step with the natural cycles of permanence and change found in the seasons. There is an anticipation that builds with the expectation of spring's new life. Summer, with its pounding heat, lays waiting just around the corner. The crisp autumn air coursing through your lungs as you soak in the deeply changing colors will surely follow. The visit of the White Wizard and his dancing snow faeries enraptures us in suspense. These all create an almost uncontrollable excitement in my soul.

At the same time, I know that life is traveling at this pace, in this rhythm, with or without me, and that the first freeze will come whether I have shut off and drained the irrigation or not. Spring will come, even if I haven't prepped the beds and started the seeds. The heat of summer will come, even if I haven't built extra shelters and accounted for more water on the pasture. Fall will arrive, even if I haven't made time to sit in its stillness with my pipe and watch the changes happen before my eyes. All this can erupt in a flutter of pain in my heart. Sometimes the Law of Life can feel like an eighteen-wheeler barreling down the side of a mountain with failed brakes, but in reality, it keeps a constant rhythm, and it is I who is either prepared for the dance or not.

But now that I have been awfully esoteric (emphasis on the awful), let me say that *Seasons at the Farm* is an attempt to capture something of the music that is made as we try to dance in step to the rhythms of the Law of Life in our little corner of the world. You will not encounter any radical calls to upend your lives and change everything you are doing. What I hope you will find instead is an ordinary joy and a humble effort to weave ourselves into the natural beauty of permanence and change in the seasons of life. I am hopeful you will be inspired to do the same.

WELCOME TO LE CHALET

 May I a small house and large garden have; And a few friends, And many books, both true. —ABRAHAM COWLEY

We moved to Le Chalet, although it didn't yet bear that name, during the winter. It was far from an ideal time to move three children, seven tons of hay, three pigs, a small herd of sheep, forty laying hens, five geese, fifty meat birds, one steer, and almost ten married years' worth of belongings. But in our desire to carve out a smallholding for ourselves, even an extremely small one by agriculture standards, we found ourselves driving back and forth between the old farm and the new farm, with a variety of farm paraphernalia in tow. Naturally, that winter was the snowiest one in more than a decade, and our old, rented farm was nestled on top of a steep gravel driveway that not even the most daring snowplow driver would attempt to clear.

At a particularly low point, as I (six months pregnant, mind you) was carrying three squawking chickens down that icy, slick driveway, I found myself tumbling down. Once the rolling stopped, I sat at the bottom of the hill and cried, still clinging to the now-snowy

birds. Maybe I didn't want a new farm this badly. Maybe I could just sit here, sulk, and somehow manage to put all the pieces back the way they were. Though, let's be honest: This was a ridiculous idea, far from the realm of possibility. You see, I'm one of those *dreamers*, one of those people who can visualize with all my senses where I want my life to go. There is one grave problem with being a dreamer, which is, when a dream takes hold, it's like stink on manure. It isn't going anywhere.

Over the course of a few weeks, we did manage to move all of our belongings, and even all the animals, to the new farm. Chaos gave way to frustration more often than I'd care to admit. Blood, sweat, and tears didn't seem enough to adequately cover the challenge of getting onto the farm. We'd been told "No!" a thousand times along the way, whether by the bank, the regulations, or the weather. But, remember now, there was *the dream*. A dream that had sunk so far into my bones, it was now inseparable from my being. Our family would have a farm of our own, come what may.

The first time I drove to the farm that would eventually become ours, not four or five days after it'd been put on the market, I messaged my husband Stuart at work saying, "Hey. This place is actually amazing. We could do something spectacular here." From that moment forward, the wheels were turning. It's as if the process of transforming this neglected, dated, and nonworking farm had already begun.

My mind danced through meadows of black-eyed Susans. I saw family members sipping iced coffee under the large pergola that would sit proudly in the courtyard. I could see wisteria creeping its way up around the kitchen door, and raised beds lined up along the north-facing orchard line. My children raced through the tall grass, and the sheep and cows grazed from the small gully that ran along the eastern side of the property.

I saw rusty buckets, transplants of hops and mint from friends planted in the potager, wind chimes, climbing roses, stone walls, and birdbaths. Like a slide-show, I could see the property room by room, acre by acre, and how it would be molded and shaped by our hands. Above all, I saw *life*. A property that had sat in slumber waiting, for us perhaps, for almost thirty years was about to be brought back to life.

We came onto the farm in the depth and despair of that frigid winter. There may have been tear stains down my dirty cheeks, but we'd made it to our farm, which we would later affection-ately call Le Chalet. Nestled on just two and a quarter hilly acres in north-central Washington, where it has sat since it was built in 1909, the cottage is surrounded by cherry and apple orchards. We know little about its history, though I'd give my right arm to hear its tales. The widow we purchased it from had owned it since the early sixties, and after her husband passed away, she'd given up producing anything on the farm. What we inherited was a small, white cottage that was desperately in need of fresh eyes, hardworking hands, and strong backs. I'd like to think that between my dear husband and myself, we could cover those bases.

We often joked that 80 percent of the battle was removing what had been left behind from decades of stylish trends and layers of decorating. No less than seven layers of flooring had been laid in the kitchen on top of the original wood-plank floor. The cedar flooring in the dining room and bedrooms had been covered up by multiple layers of carpet and paint. Oh, the stories this farm had to tell.

Le Chalet is now home to Stuart and me and our brood of four young children, Georgia, Owen, Will, and Juliette. We often joke that we are wearing this home right down to its bones. Feet trample to and fro on its wood floors each day as they run into the living room for story time or outside to the gardens for work. The home

only has three small bedrooms that are nestled together around the dining room. Originally built in the early twentieth century, the rooms are practical. Frankly, I love them just as they are. As an added perk, all roads lead to the dining room table. The design funnels the activity of the home into intimate time spent around the table. During this table time, we (and our guests) experience enriching conversation over plates of delicious, homegrown food, which it just so happens are two of my most favorite things.

Le Chalet is also home to our small barnyard of animals. There is Cecelia, our Jersey dairy cow, who helps us welcome each day with a pail of warm, frothy milk. Our small herd of breeding Katahdin sheep—Hamish,

Rosie, Noel, Gwen, Eleanor, and Gloria—keep us flush with lambs each year for meat. Also on the farm are our enormous, lazy breeding Old Spot pigs, Harry, Ginny, and Hermione, who contribute piglets to the farm each year for ham, bacon, prosciutto, and sausage. Lastly, like most smallholdings, we also keep a large flock of ducks, geese, chickens, and turkeys for eggs and poultry. These animals, along with our potager and market garden for produce, keep our bellies full for much of the year.

We wanted to cultivate a beautiful space that inspires our minds to create. Throughout our home are objects that require some skill and engagement to bring to life. For example, a secondhand baby grand piano sits in our living room, beckoning little ones to tickle its keys. Books in every form imaginable are placed here, there, and everywhere, inviting passersby with a cup of tea and five minutes to spare to explore. Stuart's guitars linger about. Art supplies are stacked on shelves, ingredients are well stocked in the kitchen, and good wine sits on the buffet in the dining room. It is a home that encourages creativity, skill, and exploration. It is, without question, my very favorite place on earth. To create a home is to create a life.

If I have one secret to share about creating a home, it's this: Learn how to create everyday magic. It is rare to find a person who can live life from one grand moment to the next, but rather, most

of our existence is tied up by what I'd call the "everyday ordinary." Life, for most of us, is not a series of red carpet events, or nights out on the town. Life is tucking your little rascals into bed at night, enjoying a glass of sparkling water during a gardening break, or reading by the fire. This is the real magic.

While we're encouraged to climb mountains, travel the world, and seek many forms of adventure, we might consider the opposite instead. What if we cultivated an existence in which we could thrive creatively, emotionally, and physically? What if our everyday life was just as magical? Through the pages of this book, I want to share my own special box of magic that I've filled over our years on the farm. It's a box filled with hot, frothy cups of espresso, sugar-dusted apple cakes, baskets of garden green beans, vintage copper pots, flannel blankets, and worn piano keys.

There is still much to be done at Le Chalet—pastures to fence, greenhouses to build, market gardens to prepare, windows to re-trim, and furniture to refinish. But for dreamers like me, who are happiest when they're cultivating beauty, the joys are endless. My husband likes to joke that our home is never the same two days in a row, as there is always a new vase of flowers to put out, a small table to move, linens to change, artwork to rearrange, or fresh paint to layer on. He's right. A home that enriches and celebrates the soul is built slowly and intentionally. It begins with a pot of primroses. A quilt. Homemade muffins.

And then the magic starts.

UNVEILING SPRING

Spring is nature's way of saying, "Let's party."
—ROBIN WILLIAMS

I've made it no secret that spring may just be my most favorite sea-son of all, though I'm sure that's not being fair to the others. It's the tantalizing scent of soil after a long winter that intoxicates me. The earth begins to reawaken, and I'm more than eager to witness the rebirth.

Years ago, when Stuart and I were newly married and living in a rundown rental house, we welcomed a young gentleman friend of ours over for a quiet lunch after church. We dished up smoked salmon, a lemon-infused pasta, and a small bowl of local berries. We sat out on our decrepit, pale blue porch (always littered with garden tools and garbage), and though the scenery left much to be desired, the three of us soaked up the first of spring's rays and felt for the first time in a long time as if we were thawing from the inside out. We basked all afternoon in the comforting sun, talking about our hopes and intentions for the coming days. That is what spring gives us: hope for what is ahead.

Spring is when we set expectations for the growing season. There's no garden patch too big to plant, no flower too finicky to survive your brown thumb. Perhaps this is the year, finally, that you'll remember to trellis your tomatoes in the spring before they explode in the summer sun. Or perhaps this is the year you'll welcome a small flock of Peking ducks onto the farm. Dream big! Spring is the time for ruthless ambitions.

My spring dreams allow me to visualize a farm that is free of feed bags and twine and bathed in wildflowers and fruiting trees. You see, in the spring, I'm permitted to be less concerned with reality. Rather, I'm allowed to daydream about the long, warm days ahead and what that will mean for the farm. Many of the seeds and projects that are planned and planted now won't be fully realized until the summer or fall, so it's a time when I can hope with abandon that my goals will easily come to fruition. Spring allows us to visualize things that live somewhere between magazine pages, online searches, and home-improvement television shows. It's all going to be perfect. And magical. And beautiful. And amen.

Traditionally, this time of the year inspires "spring cleaning." Magazines often tell us that spring is a time of neutral colors, organized houses, and egg wreaths. That's certainly not true on our farm. More often than not, we head inside covered in mud and manure. Long before any green grass has time to protect the soil from heavy rains, we are eager to sink our fingers and toes into the dirt after a long winter. For farmers, it's almost impossible to stay away from the land that feeds our bodies and souls. While others may spend the chilly days of early spring organizing closets and donating unused items from the toy bin, farmers are bent over in the garden bed, tilling in manure and planting the earliest spinach varieties their climate allows. Though the flies and sweat have yet to make their appearance, spring is dirty in its own special way.

That's not to say that the farmer isn't also purging the weight of winter. Spring will often find the farmer raking deep mulch off overwintered carrots, burning up old Christmas tree limbs, and scraping out a few frozen months' worth of manure from the animal shelter. With that shedding of winter weight, the farmer is able to welcome the *joy of life* back to the farm. Before long, the robin calls from the garden bed. The first bugs begin to make themselves known. Spring branches are eagerly tucked into glass jars for the dining room table.

Beyond the farm and home, we are also more than eager to welcome spring's early life back onto our plates and into our bellies. The frozen vegetables, cured meats, and dried fruits faithfully saw us through the bleak depths of a cold winter, but by spring, our palates are certainly ready for subtler and lighter flavors. Asparagus soufflés for breakfast are far more welcome than another bowl of

oatmeal. Baby greens allow us to make salad upon salad, topped only with spicy early-spring radishes and a drizzle of vinegar. Thanks to chilly winds and nights, soup is still the perfect way to highlight the first flavors of the season (not to mention an easy supper to fix after a long day spent in the garden).

Can I let you in on another culinary favorite of mine in the spring? Espresso. I find that this hot, rich drink is an absolute must to counter the sometimes cold and tedious work the farm requires each spring. To stand in the fresh air with a cup in hand, looking out over the land to be tended, is nourishment for the spirit (and belly).

Spring vegetables. Dreams. Espresso. This, my friends, is where the magic is made.

The Spring Garden

 Spring won't let me stay in this house any longer! I must get out and breathe the air deeply again. —*GUSTAV MAHLER*

If there's anything that'll get a farmgirl's heart giddy in the spring, it's a slew of flowering bulbs strewn around the farmhouse. Hyacinths, tulips, crocuses, and the ever-popular daffodil bring cottage charm to any table and can easily be moved around and shifted to whatever space or place setting you've got. They can be used to decorate for a special feast with friends or can be imperfectly gathered on your breakfast table while you enjoy morning omelets with the family. In my humble opinion, *they're simply perfect*. Rustic. Charming. Proof of the life that is bursting forth! I'm pretty set on the fact that every seasonal table requires some living, floral highlights.

Potted spring bulbs can be utilized indoors or outdoors, depending on your space and desires. I like to keep some inside for a striking spring visual, as well as have larger pots of planted bulbs outside in our courtyard. They're always eager to bring the party, and after a long, gray winter, I'm more than happy to see their faces.

INDOOR BULB PLANTERS

Most indoor bulbs are easy to grow, but do require some fore-thought to get them to bloom. It's best to begin the process of planting indoor bulb planters in the fall. Why? Many bulbs are native to cooler climates and are acclimated to a time of rest during the winter. Because bulbs would naturally be planted in the garden soil outside where they would lie dormant until spring, they require us to trick them ever so slightly to get them to actually bloom in our artificial indoor environment. Daffodils, tulips, hyacinths, and crocuses are all bulbs that require chilling in order to bloom. To achieve these indoor blooms, here are the steps to follow:

1. Choose a container that allows the bulbs at least 3 inches of room under the planted bulb for root growth.

2. Fill the container with potting soil to about 2 inches below the rim of the container.

3. Cluster the bulbs into the middle of the pot. This will help create a natural-appearing cluster of flowers. Because chill and bloom times are different for each flower, it's best to stick with one variety per pot.

4. Top each container off with compost mixture, water thoroughly, and label with the planting date and bulb variety.

5. Store the containers in an area of your home that can be kept at around 40°F. This could be a basement, a garage, a barn, or a refrigerator. Anywhere dark and cool will do the trick. The containers should remain at this temperature for at least sixteen weeks. Periodically check the containers, ensuring that they're adequately moist but not wet.

6. After the cooling period, the containers can be removed and allowed to sit in a mild, dark area of your home. After a few weeks, they can be moved to a sunny window. Be gentle with them as they wake up from a long winter slumber!

PLANTING GUIDE

For blooms in **JANUARY**,
plant bulbs in early **SEPTEMBER**.

For blooms in **FEBRUARY**,
plant bulbs in early **OCTOBER**.

For blooms in **MARCH**,
plant bulbs in early **NOVEMBER**.

For blooms in **APRIL**, look out
the window!

AGING TERRACOTTA POTS

Potted bulbs, and a variety of other spring flowers, look absolutely perfect tucked into aged terracotta pots. But have you ever priced out the antique versions of these popular pots? Yowza. To counter those hefty price tags, here's a cheater's method I've used to get that same gorgeous patina that comes with a real vintage version.

1 pound hydrated lime, available at your local home-improvement store

1 quart water

¼ pound salt

Steel wool pad

Terracotta pots of various shapes and sizes.

In a large bowl or bucket, mix the hydrated lime with water. The consistency should be that of a thick paste.

Add the salt. Stir again to combine.

Add more water, if needed, to get the whitewash to the viscosity of a thick soup.

To age the pots, use a paintbrush to roughly paint the surface of the terracotta pot with the whitewash in a single layer. Don't be clean with your lines; it's time to be a bit sloppy and carefree. Allow the pot to dry.

After the pot has dried, use a steel wool pad to buff and scuff up the pot until it looks aged to your liking.

You can use the pots immediately for planting or let them sit outside in your garden for more patina.

SPRING MOSS

Last February, I bought myself a present. I'd spent far too many days staring out the icy windows at the hellacious landscape. We'd been under snow since November, and by late winter, I'd about lost myself in the icy cold. Stuart brought me a package that had just been delivered. I eagerly tore open the box, and before I even caught a glimpse of what lay inside, I could smell it. *Earth.* What was packaged so carefully was five pounds of rain forest moss from the nearby Olympic Peninsula. Just over the other side of our beloved Cascade Mountains was a forest still alive and green.

Keeping moss on hand, whether ordered online or from a garden store (or even harvested from your own local forest) is a wonderful way to bring things to life in early spring when it's just *not quite there yet.*

Uses for Moss Indoors

Live moss is easy to care for and only requires a slight spritzing of water, on the surface, once or twice a week. The moss should be kept out of direct sunlight if you'd like it to keep living. Otherwise, let it dry up—it looks almost just as beautiful!

Cover the base of your indoor plants. The moss will help retain moisture in the soil and make the plants look nice and fresh after a season of low light and chilled air.

Make a living centerpiece. Moss is easily pliable and lends itself well to being shaped to fit your tablescape. Blend it with a few potted flowers or branches for an easy spring feel.

Build an indoor terrarium. Terrariums have become popular again and are easy to make and maintain. Mosses are an essential ingredient.

HOMEMADE TERRARIUMS

Terrariums are little microenvironments that are created in clear glass containers. Multiple species of mosses can be added to the containers for variation of color, texture, and life!

Sealable glass container or glass dome

Peat moss

Moss, air plants, succulents, ferns, or orchids

Variety of rocks, twigs, branches, birds' nests, or decor of choice

Fill your container ⅓ full with peat moss. If using a glass dome, find a bowl or pot that will fit inside your dome.

Arrange the plants, tucking them into the peat moss, so they vary a bit in height and look as if they were growing naturally.

Layer your mosses around the base of your plants so that they also vary in textures and colors.

Layer in the additional decor, such as rocks and twigs, as it pleases you. Have fun as you build your little forest. Fortunately, terrariums are very forgiving.

Spritz your plants and mosses with water and place the dome over the top or the top on the container. The terrarium will begin to "sweat" and leave little moisture droplets inside the glass. *It's magical—enjoy it!* The terrarium should be spritzed a few times a week with water and kept slightly moist, but not wet. You can fluff it up as needed by changing out plants, layering in more moss, or adding more decor.

TENDING TO INDOOR PLANTS

Through the late winter and early spring, I tend to collect more indoor plants than is socially acceptable. Sometimes I kill them almost instantly, despite my best efforts. Other times, the plants will live for years and years with little to no care on my part.

Years ago, on one of our wedding anniversaries, Stuart surprised me with a 5-foot fiddle-leaf tree. It could've been a diamond given the level of my excitement, because as far as this farmgirl is concerned, trees are just as valuable. I won't say that it's been kept up perfectly. Often, I forget to water it until its leaves begin to droop and look slightly depressed. A bit of water perks it up, though I'm sure what it would really love is a transplant into a new pot, a bit of fertilizer,

MY FAVORITE PLANTS FOR INDOOR SPACES:

Clover	Palm
Fiddle-leaf tree	Mother-in-law tongue
Herbs	
Orchids	Succulents
Philodendron	Peace lily
Pothos	Jade

some fresh moss mulch, and perhaps a good dusting (little cobwebs always find their way between its large, flat leaves). The fiddle-leaf has been a welcome addition to wherever I put it and is a sweet reminder of a man who knows my language of love: plants.

When spring is knocking at your door, give yourself full permission to fill every corner of your home with something *fresh* and *green*. It will give you hope and inspiration for the days ahead!

THE RETURN OF THE GARDEN

Though I slave away in my gardens, I'm admittedly a bit of a lazy gardener. Perennials make up about 80 percent of what I plant, so I only have to tend to them carefully for a year or two before they

are able to fend for themselves. This not only keeps the garden filled in and lush, but also makes it easier for me to focus on the vegetables. The vegetables are extremely important to us (you know, on account of them being *food* and all that), so I'm keen to give them a bit more of my attention than the cutting flowers.

As spring would always have it, I buy whatever annuals or blooms are available at the nursery, even if it's far too cold for them to be planted just quite yet. I can't help myself! Can you?

After the initial chill of spring has passed, and full-on spring

planting mode has begun, it's go time. This is not a time for the faint of heart on the farm. After all, teeny little onion starts must be transplanted one by one . . . row by row . . . hour by hour. Radish seeds are sown, quite casually because radishes are easygoing like that, between the much-harder-to-please carrot seeds. Much of the spring days are spent bent over, raking beds, and digging small trenches to plant seeds here, there, and everywhere. All of this is done with the belief that once again, the sun, soil, and water will work their magic, and these tiny little seeds will explode and become the sustenance of the farm. It is an act of hope.

DIY SEED MARKERS

I used to think that seed markers were a waste of time; that is, until I started broccoli, kale, cauliflower, and cabbages all in the same tray one year and ended up with a hodgepodge of plantings in the potager from misidentified seedlings. I've since learned my lesson and always incorporate seed markers not only for their aesthetic charm, but also for their practicality in identifying newly planted rows (particularly for visitors who aren't as familiar). My gardener friend Grace takes it a step further and labels her rows with the particular variety being grown, so she can easily size up its performance next to the others.

You can get as creative (or practical) as you'd like with your seed markers, but if I'm going to incorporate something into the garden, I want it to be beautiful! Here are a few easy and inexpensive ways to make your own:

Wine corks. Because we all need an excuse to drink a few more bottles, no?

Broken bits of pottery. I have broken plates and mugs in a planter outside my kitchen door just waiting patiently to be painted on. This gives me a reason to reuse some of those pieces I still love.

Wooden spoons. I collect vintage wooden spoons, but for these markers, I just use the cheap ones from the grocery store. They'll weather and warp soon enough in the sun.

EDIBLE PERENNIALS

I'll never forget the first perennial plant I was given. In our very first house together, Stuart and I built a small raised garden bed along the property's fence line that we shared with the neighbor.

We would make small talk over the tall fence as we'd both tend to our garden beds.

One afternoon, while I was harvesting the peppers, I saw a small black container poke up over the top of the fence. I grabbed the container and peeked inside. "What is it?" I asked. "Rhubarb!" my neighbor responded. "Don't you ever eat rhubarb?" "Guess I will now!" I laughed, embarrassed to admit that I had no idea what rhubarb was. We ended up moving from the house before we ever got to see that rhubarb grow. I'd like to think that whoever lives there now is enjoying its bounty. A house with a berry patch or—*gasp!*—a fruit tree is better than money in the bank.

MY EDIBLE PERENNIAL FAVORITES

Rhubarb

Asparagus

Strawberries

Apricots

Horseradish

Herbs (particularly chives)

Raspberries

Gooseberries

I have a perennial problem. The problem being, of course, that I plant far too many of them. The fact that you can plant them just once and reap their bounty for years (even decades) feels too amazing to be real. Spring perennials are among the best to offer up the gentle, fresh flavors of the season.

PERENNIAL FLOWERS

It took me ages to learn the names of flowers. In my days at the flower shop, I'd often wave a stem at my boss, asking, "What's this called again?" or ask her to "hand me some of that whatcha-diggit over there." She continually reminded me of their names, which would eventually become so familiar, their mention would be like reuniting with an old friend.

My relationship with those flowers carried over to our first farm, where I built up over 2,000 square feet of beds devoted to flowers.

The lavender was shipped from a local farm, daisies were transplanted from my aunt's backyard, honeysuckle climbed the chicken coop, and succulents crept along the garden stones. We spent hours bent over in those garden beds, digging holes, burying root balls, and praying that the plants would survive.

And you know what? They did! That second year, they came back with amazing beauty. And then, as life goes, we moved away from our first perennial garden that next fall. I wept. Literally. I couldn't bear the thought of leaving behind these flowers that I'd chosen, loved, and nurtured for the first few years of their life. As Stuart calmed my rattled emotions, I remember actually saying to him that to move away from the gardens felt like abandoning them.

The pain eventually passed as I drank extra honey lattes and worked tirelessly to build and beautify the empty spaces at our new farm. Though the gardens are uniquely different, I'm happy to be building a beautiful future with "new friends" here. Each garden serves as a blank canvas, awaiting the expression of its holder to burst forth in creativity. Each time one gets to experience that surge of creativity and inspiration is reason for celebration.

Many of my potager gardens here are built around perennial flowers. While I enjoy gardening, I also enjoy the magic that comes in the spring when flowers planted years prior begin to push up from the soil and greet the sunshine with open leaves and blooms. Though I layer in a few annuals each year, the foundation of our flower beds undoubtedly revolves around a deep love affair with those flowers that willingly come back year after year. There are a few perennials that particularly strike me as cottage flowers and ones that I was eager to incorporate here on the farm. They are the accessories—the makeup, if you will—of a home's exterior. All the more reason to take the time and effort to make your beds beautiful.

MY PERENNIAL FLOWER FAVORITES

Echinacea	Yarrow
Hollyhocks	Foxglove
Lady's mantle	Poppies
Salvia	Sage
Lavender	Bachelor buttons
Hydrangeas	
Peonies	Bee balm
Roses	Lilacs
Crocuses	Elderberries
Lilies	Bellflower
Tulips	Columbine
Daisies	Coral bells
Phlox	Lupines
Delphinium	Dianthus

PRESSING FLOWERS

Pressing flowers is an old way of preserving the fragile beauty of blooms. I've taken on a habit of pressing flowers and herbs to tuck inside cookbooks or special novels that we read with the children. I like to think of them flipping through the pages with their own children and finding tangible reminders of the farm and their childhood. Our older daughter, Georgia, presses her own for a variety of art projects and has been known to tape them around the house where they don't belong.

Flowers of any kind
Paper towels
Wax paper
Heavy books

Select the flowers you'd like to press and clean them of any debris or bugs. Snip them down to a size that will fit inside a book.

Lay the flower on a paper towel and lay another paper towel over the top. The paper towels will absorb moisture from the flower to prevent it from causing mold on the blossom.

Sandwich the paper towels between two pieces of wax paper, which will prevent any moisture from leaching onto the pages of the book.

Place the entire flower sandwich between the pages of a heavy book and close the book. Add five or so additional heavy books on top of the first book and allow the stack to sit undisturbed for two weeks.

Remove the flower carefully from the book and enjoy!

Rosemary is historically sent to let someone know you're thinking of them. Add a pressed rosemary sprig or two in the next letter or present you send.

WHAT WE'RE GROWING
ON THE FARM

I can't think about a spring garden without remembering my Grandpa Telford. He would meticulously plan his garden to achieve maximum productivity and taste. Though his garden plot was just a little dirt patch on the side of his redbrick garage, it was a special space for him (and his grandkids). He would sink posts into the ground and connect them with string to ensure that his lines of tomatoes and corn were planted perfectly straight. If he could see my scattered rows, piles of weeds, and rubbish, I'm sure he would chuckle.

Spring is certainly not a time for the gardener to be lazy. Not only are seeds planted for the early-spring harvests, but seeds and starts are also planted for all of the crops to come in the hot months of summer. Though specific last-frost dates in the United States are set by specific zones and thus planting dates vary slightly, what's growing in the spring garden is relatively universal. Here's what you'd find in ours:

Beets. This past year, I went to "beet school" and learned from an organic farmer how to grow them better. For beets, this involves giving the seeds plenty of space to germinate and grow. Once I learned to thin my beets (one beet seedling for every 4–5 inches of growing space), they began to grow much larger and more uniformly. Detroit Dark Red, Bull's Blood, and Chioggia have done well for me through the years.

Broccoli. Some years broccoli grows better than others, so I've learned to be unattached to the outcome. It's times like these

on the farm that one can be thankful for farmers' markets and farming friends. The years I have been successful in my broccoli growing, De Cicco was the variety that helped me through.

Cabbages. When harvested in the late spring, cabbage heads are less tightly wound than those left to grow into the summer months. These are ideal for sautéing in a few tablespoons of butter with a pinch of sea salt until soft and slightly golden. When in doubt, plant more cabbages! Copenhagen Market and Mammoth Red have both been great growers in our garden. They're ideal for storage, eating fresh, and even turning into sauerkraut.

Green onions. There are a million wonderful varieties that will provide you with a gentle zing of onion flavor. Grow a ton! Extras can be chopped and stored in the freezer.

Onions. I grow enough onions each year on the farm for us to use two a day, every day. That's a lot of onions. Because I store mine through the winter in the root cellar, I opt to grow mostly varieties that will keep. Yellow of Parma has always done well for me and stores reliably well. For eating fresh through the summer, it's Walla Walla Sweets (hey, I'm from Washington State!).

Peas. Eagerly climbing up garden gates and trellises, peas are some of the first seeds to be planted in the chilly soil each spring. There are varieties where you can eat the entire pod, like Amish Snap, and others that require shelling the peas, such as British Wonder. Plant both, for good measure.

Radishes. French Breakfast, Early Scarlet Globe, and Holmes Royal Red are my personal favorites. Plant a fresh row of radishes every two weeks in the early spring for a long harvest season.

Shallots. My favorites are the French Grey shallots planted in the fall, alongside my garlic, and harvested in the spring. Every year I grow more and more and more . . .

Spring greens. For months, we've been enjoying meats, beets, carrots, cabbages, potatoes, sauerkraut, jams, jellies, and other preserves and stored produce. But as the first of the spring spinach begins to be harvested, the fresh flavor is almost more than I can handle. The subtle greens of spring refresh our taste buds. Bonus: They're incredibly easy to grow and mighty prolific, which means you'll get to enjoy greens (lots of them!) for weeks and weeks. Plant spinach, mustard greens, kale, collard greens, arugula, lettuce, and Swiss chard every few weeks for continual harvesting.

Spring Recipes

Where was all the food? Dear folks, the food was in homes,
gardens, local fields, and forests. It was near kitchens, near tables,
near bedsides. It was in the pantry, the cellar, the backyard.
—*JOEL SALATIN*

By spring, I've eaten the last of the onions in winter storage and
am most likely sick of frozen fruit. Winter days lend themselves to
heavier meals and denser breads, but this fare is quickly replaced
when the first pea pods and garlic scapes arrive. There's a new apron
for the cook and a fresh bouquet for the kitchen counter, even if it's
just the first few green tree branches. It's time to celebrate because
it's *fun* to finally have something fresh to eat again.

On my yearlong farming calendar, there is truly not a day more
anticipated than when I slip on my wool socks and knee-high wel-
lies, and venture out to the chilly wasteland of a garden only to find
what I swore would never return: the very first green leaves of my
perennials poking out of the spring soil.

I usually celebrate with champagne and more cheese and chocolate than should be allowed. Because it's *that* special of a day.

STRAWBERRY AND MINT MIMOSAS

These mimosas look *divine* on the table. Planting strawberries was one of the very first tasks I set for myself on our farm, and though I only got about ten plants in before the summer passed, I did it! Only 500 more linear feet to plant and then, just maybe, I'll be satisfied. Oh well. I suppose I always have mimosas to get me through. **Serves 4**

1 cup organic garden strawberries

2 tablespoons maple syrup or honey

Handful of mint leaves

Champagne

Combine the strawberries and maple syrup in a bowl. Use the back of a fork to smoosh them together until the strawberries are completely broken down. This can also be done in a blender or food processor for a smoother puree.

Add 1 tablespoon of the strawberry mixture to a champagne flute.

Gently bruise a few mint leaves in your hand before putting them into the champagne flute. This will help release the oils and bring out the fragrance.

Top the flute off with champagne and serve immediately.

SPRING EGG OMELET

When I was learning to make omelets, I consulted a cookbook written ages ago. The author was Irish, cooked her omelets until hard, and was disgusted by the softer, more pillowy French version. She made it clear her omelets would not "weep" as theirs did. Let's assume this spring egg omelet is somewhere in the middle.

This omelet is always best in spring, when the chicken eggs are at their finest. The weather is mild, the grass is green, and the bugs are plenty. Our spring egg yolks are deep orange and always stand tall and firm (a sign of freshness), which means in the busy spring, there is a whole heck of a lot of omelets being made. **Serves 1**

Melt the butter in a 10-inch skillet. My preference for omelets is a cast-iron skillet because of the heat distribution and weight. Allow the skillet to get hot as the butter melts.

Meanwhile, mix the eggs, cream, and sea salt in a bowl. Whisk until well combined.

Pour the eggs into the skillet and immediately begin to move them around. The point is not to scramble them, but rather to keep the mixture from sticking to the bottom of the skillet. Keep this up for about 15 seconds before sprinkling the cheese over the eggs and popping a lid on the skillet for 1 minute. Turn the heat down to low.

Remove the lid and fold the omelet over itself before transferring it carefully to a plate. Garnish with fresh herbs.

1 tablespoon butter

2 eggs

3 tablespoons cream or whole milk

Pinch of sea salt

2 tablespoons grated cheese of your choice

Fresh herbs, for garnish

PEA SOUP WITH HERBS

This is a far cry from the heavy split-pea soup of wintertime! It highlights one of spring's big players—the fresh pea—and gives it a chance to shine at center stage. It's one of our children's favorites and often requested, even if peas aren't in season. Don't worry, frozen petite peas work as well. **Serves 4**

3 tablespoons olive oil

4 shallots

2 cups small, dried pasta shells

5 cups chicken or vegetable stock

Sea salt and freshly ground black pepper, to taste

4 cups fresh or frozen petite peas

Chopped parsley and mint, for garnish

Toasted pumpkin seeds, for garnish

Heat the olive oil in a soup pot. Peel and mince the shallots and sauté them in the olive oil for 2–3 minutes, until just soft.

Add the pasta and stock and bring to a simmer. Continue cooking the pasta until it is cooked al dente. Season the broth to taste with salt and pepper.

Add the peas and cook for 4–5 minutes, until the peas are just tender and warm. Again, season to taste with salt.

Garnish each bowl of soup with a generous sprinkling of freshly chopped parsley and mint, and a good pinch of the pumpkin seeds. Serve immediately so the peas don't get wrinkly. Nobody wants wrinkly peas, man.

SPRING GREENS WITH LEMON

Spring greens need hardly any additional ingredients. In the spring, they're young, tender, and subtle in flavor. I'm a big advocate for enjoying food in its simplest form, when it's at its peak. This recipe is a perfect example of that. Use whatever greens you have growing in the garden. **Serves 6**

4 cups spring greens of choice, washed and finely sliced

1 cup water

Zest of 1 lemon

Juice of ½ lemon

2 tablespoons olive oil

Large pinch of sea salt

Place the greens in a large pan. Pour in the water, cover, and bring to a simmer. Allow the greens to steam for 3–4 minutes, until just tender. Drain the greens, using a colander, before transferring them to a serving bowl.

Add the lemon zest, lemon juice, olive oil, and sea salt to the greens. Toss to combine. Enjoy!

GARLIC SCAPE PESTO

Most people know of garlic, but have yet to experience the blessing of garlic scapes. Each spring, while the garlic bulb grows underground, a pointy scape will shoot up into the sky. These scapes are cut from the garlic, so that the energy from the plant will go into producing a large bulb versus a flower. The gardener is left with a bucket of garlic scapes that are completely worthy of their own pesto. It's perfectly delicious over pasta, potatoes, or grilled vegetables. **Serves 8**

Place the garlic scapes, pine nuts, and Parmesan cheese in a food processor. Blend to combine until the mixture resembles coarse sand, scraping down the sides as necessary.

Add the lemon juice, sea salt, and black pepper. Blend to combine.

While the food processor is running slowly, drizzle in the olive oil, until the mixture is combined and smooth. Store in the refrigerator.

20 garlic scapes

1 cup pine nuts or almonds

1 cup shredded Parmesan cheese

Juice of 1 lemon

Large pinch of sea salt

½ teaspoon freshly ground black pepper

⅔ cup olive oil

ELDERFLOWER CORDIAL

Elderflowers are widely celebrated in our part of the country. The wild, perennial elderberry bushes pepper the hillsides all around, and when they come into flower throughout the spring, it's like a million little stars coming out to celebrate. This cordial is easy to make and captures the *essence* of those little flowers—an earthy, lightly citrusy, floral delight. Serve it over ice cream, in a cocktail, or even over pancakes. **Serves 18**

15 elderflower clusters

4 cups honey

4 cups filtered water

Zest and juice of 2 lemons

Wash the elderflower clusters and set them aside to dry.

Combine the honey and water in a pot over medium-low heat. Allow the ingredients to melt together, stirring as necessary.

Gently pluck the flowers from the elderflower clusters and add them to the pot, along with the lemon zest and juice. Cover the pot, turn off the heat, and allow the cordial to infuse for 24 hours before straining it and bottling. Store in the refrigerator; the cordial will keep well here for months.

SPRING ASPARAGUS BUNDLES

Although asparagus can be pickled for winter eating, it's most pleasurable in the spring when the fresh, crisp stalks are plucked from the ground. I always find that asparagus bundles are an extra-special way to enjoy its understated flavor. **Serves 6**

2 pounds fresh asparagus

6 strips bacon

4 tablespoons maple syrup

4 tablespoons butter, melted

Pinch of sea salt

Freshly ground black pepper

Preheat the oven to 425°F.

Snap the ends off the asparagus (they will naturally break where the stem gets tough). Divide the asparagus into 12 bundles with roughly 6–8 spears in each bundle.

Cut each bacon strip in half. Precook the bacon in a skillet until it's mostly cooked but still pliable.

Wrap a strip of bacon around each asparagus bundle, taking care to not overlap the bacon.

Lay the bundles on a baking sheet, bacon seam-side down, and drizzle them with the maple syrup and butter. Use your fingers to gently move the bundles around and coat them in the butter and syrup.

Sprinkle the bundles with salt and a bit of pepper. Bake in the oven for 5–10 minutes until the bacon is thoroughly cooked and the asparagus is tender but still crisp.

HONEY-SWEETENED STRAWBERRY-RHUBARB JAM

The most coveted of all jams around the farm, due to our lack of large strawberry harvests, is always strawberry-rhubarb. We sweeten ours with honey from our own beehives because the flavor of honey plays so nicely with the fruit. **Serves 12**

Combine the strawberries, rhubarb, lemon juice, and honey in a large stockpot. Bring the mixture to a gentle simmer and cook for 10–15 minutes, until the fruit begins to dissolve into a liquid.

Remove the pot from the burner, stir in the pectin according to package directions, and put the pot back on the stove. Bring the jam up to a boil for 10 additional minutes.

Remove the pot from the heat and let it sit for a few minutes while you gather and wash your jam jars.

Ladle the jam into the jars and secure the lids. Process in a water-canner, according to the manufacturer's instructions, for 10 minutes before removing the jars and setting them on a flat surface while they cool and seal. Alternatively, the jam can be cooled and ladled into plastic containers and stored in the freezer.

8 cups strawberries, stems removed

8 cups rhubarb stems, chopped into 1-inch pieces

4 tablespoons lemon juice

2 cups honey

3 teaspoons low-sugar pectin

Spring in the Home

In the spring, at the end of the day, you should smell like dirt.
—MARGARET ATWOOD

My husband grew up in Georgia, and every year he would spend the holidays at his grandmother's home. She was a traditional woman who took Christmas very, *very* seriously. So seriously, in fact, that she had a different tree, with a different theme, in each room of her home. Each one was decorated from top to bottom with elaborate ribbons, ornaments, and sparkle. I'm sure our first Christmas tree together, decorated in foraged pinecones and secondhand ornaments, fell a bit short of Stuart's expectations.

But really, that's just how things are in our home. We live in it, day in and day out. It's not a special place that we visit on long weekends or only after working a long day at the office. Our family of six lives in every inch of our 1909 farmhouse, and thus every inch of that space is valuable real estate for what fills it. This is why I have a tendency to decorate for the seasons very gently. I like to focus instead on bringing a few spring essentials into our home that lift our spirits and create an inspiring and uplifting environment.

SPRING TEXTILES

I'm not a designer, but I do have an absolute obsession for balance and contrast of textures. Part of the farmhouse feel is completely based on texture. Cottages are often built from old lumber, stucco, stone, metal, cedar shakes, and hay thatching. It's a textural delight to the eyes! These rough textures work beautifully alongside the soft, comfortable feel of spring textiles.

Strip Down

And not just your winter sweaters. The first step in freshening up your home for spring is to spend a few hours just *stripping down* the excess that has accumulated over the winter. The best palette is a blank palette, and it's often helpful for us to imagine our space in a new way when we're able to see the bones of it more easily.

A great place to start is to remove all pillows, throws, and coffee-table decor from a room. Stack it all in a separate corner and assess the entire space without them. What colors do you see? What textures?

Bring Out the White Linens

White linens are a farmhouse staple. I have a modest collection of vintage linens that I've acquired from sellers in France, Belgium, and England. The cloth is richly textured, with a homemade feeling. I can't help but run my fingertips over it and daydream about covering a spring picnic table with it or that ratty old chair that sits in my dining room. Linen has a magical way of feeling *slightly* sophisticated, and yet romantically wrinkly and rustic all at the same time. It's comfortable, but structured. And it's the perfect fabric to bring into your space when you're not sure which direction to go. White linen curtains? *Come on!*

Available from online markets such as Etsy, vintage farmhouse linens often come embroidered with the initials of whomever used it before it landed in your lucky hands.

Bring Out the Burlap

Beautifully textured burlap is also a staple in farmhouse decor. Woven out of fibers from the jute plant, burlap bags have long been used on the farm to hold everything from hay to grain to beans to animal fodder. Burlap use soon expanded beyond the barnyard and into the home. It's not a cuddly fabric (burlap sheets, anyone?), but it sure does have that farmhouse feel. Couple that with its durability and strength, and it's the perfect fabric to stand up to little farmboys who like to play "indoor sledding" down the stairs with Mama's throw pillows.

Burlap can be used to make curtains, dress up old pots, cover decorative throw pillows, or as a rustic tablecloth for an outdoor dining space. The light brown color lends itself well to the muted, earthy shades of spring.

Bring Out the Florals

Don't worry. I'm not talking about your grandmother's florals . . .
or even your mother's florals. *Shudder*. But let's not throw the baby
out with the bathwater just because of some bad taste. Floral textiles,
done correctly, can be absolutely dreamy. Obviously, as the flowers
begin to bloom in the garden, bringing out floral textiles naturally
extends this into your home.

I'm often surprised how prevalent floral patterns (think curtains,
pillows, and bedding) are in traditional cottage and European decor.

COTTAGE ELEMENTS FOR SPRING

In addition to textiles, I like to change things up each season with
small accents such as plates, containers, and other pretty things. It's
also a good time to rethink how things are displayed and whether
that could use some refreshing as well.

White Ironstone

Picture a large china cabinet in the dining room. It's rustic and
shabby and oh-so-fabulous. What do you see stacked inside it? My
guess is that, if you're at all familiar with farmhouse decor, it's stacks
and stacks of white ironstone. I know you know what I'm talkin'
about—those striking white pitchers, plates, bowls, serving platters,
and gravy boats all mismatched together in a display of imperfect
farmhouse charm. Ironstone is about as cottage as it gets.

Readily available and popular in the nineteenth century, ironstone was an alternative to easily chipped porcelain and was a staple in farmhouses, where wear and tear on kitchen equipment was common. Nowadays, you can easily pick up vintage ironstone online, at estate sales, or at secondhand stores. If the price tag is too big a bother, stock up on thick white plates from your local home store, display them with a few all-white antique pieces, and call it a day. It'll still pull off the look wonderfully well. The more mismatched and stacked, the better.

Open Shelving

Part of cottage charm is baring the house's soul to its guests. Not a lot is hidden in cottages. There aren't man-caves or hidden passageways. Cottages are often small, and thus their contents tend to

be very public. This trait forces me to be intentional with what comes into my space and what it looks like (it's hard to hide hot pink beanbags in a farmhouse). Open shelving was a common element in old farmhouses, when cabinets were elaborate and expensive. Instead of hiding dishes and ingredients behind closed doors, open shelving allows you to put on display the very contents of your home that you find endearing.

Spring is a beautiful time to strip away the unnecessary items from open shelves and refresh the space as you move things from here to there, dust off the contents, refill the spice and grain jars, and add a few new pieces or plants to soften the space for the season. Here are some tips for beautiful open shelves:

Balance textures. Incorporate items that are wood, metal, glass, and ironstone for depth and interest.

Mix old and new. If your shelves are filled with only antiques, it won't be believable that you actually use the space. Instead, incorporate new and old items. Vintage crocks that store flour can be coupled with stashes of new wine glasses, for example.

Gather baskets. An array of baskets is an inexpensive way to store odds and ends that need to be gathered or hidden. These can be stacked on shelves, tucked under cabinets, hung from the ceiling, or placed on countertops.

Always incorporate glass. Glass is remarkably timeless and always looks clean and relevant, no matter the design style of your space. Glass can be incorporated by adding drinking vessels, spice jars, or baking dishes.

More copper. Copper offers a warm color to your space. Unlike stainless steel, which tends to read more industrial and sterile, copper offers a patina that is unique every day and offers a welcoming touch to open shelving.

Cluster like items together. Items always have the greatest impact when they're clustered together. "Three's a collection," so if you've got a few crocks, gather them together for maximum visual appeal. Same goes for wine bottles, stockpots, knives, ramekins, and so on.

Open shelving requires a bit more attention than cabinets. After all, we love our open shelving for the eye candy it brings to our kitchens! Take a bit of time to really feel out how you use your kitchen and what needs to be placed where on the shelves, according to necessity. After the essentials are in place, fill in the gaps with the fun stuff!

Galvanized Buckets

Part of spring's magic comes from bringing elements of the outdoors in and the indoors out. It reminds us that, once again, we'll be able to live outside soon, no longer captives to our cozy homes. Galvanized buckets do just that.

On the farm, we use these buckets to feed our livestock grain, gather eggs, collect tomatoes from the garden, plant bulbs, and hold potatoes in the kitchen. They get old, beat up, and collect dents, but despite the wear, they actually seem to get better with age. They can be picked up new at your local feed store and left to grow some patina with regular usage. Or, if you're impatient like me, you can usually find them sitting outside your local antiques store, gathering cobwebs and dried leaves in their bottoms. Grab as many as you can, snag a latte on your way home, and get creative! When in doubt, stick a plant in it.

Silk Flowers

Before the flower garden gives us an abundance of summer blooms, we can *fake it till we make it*. Sourcing some top-notch silk flowers will bring the hope of what's to come into our living spaces. Silk flowers have come a *long* way since I was a florist over fifteen years ago and are now almost impossible to tell from real blossoms (apart from the fragrance, of course). I keep a few bunches of bloom-ing branches, roses, and tulips on hand so that I always have "fresh" flowers to dress up the cottage. Here are a few tips on silk flowers:

- They're most believable when they're bunched together in a mass. So gather together five to ten stems of the same type when incorporating them into your room.

- Display them in vintage jars, pitchers, crocks, or bottles for maximum farmhouse charm. This will also disguise the fact that they're not in water like real flowers would be!

- Keep the amount you use tasteful. Too much of anything is a bit tacky in the farmhouse, so downplay their awesomeness.

- When it's time to put them away for the season, wrap the entire bunch in tissue paper and tie it with string. This will keep the flowers from getting dirty in storage and won't squish their distinct shape.

PAINTED FARMHOUSE FLOORS

When we arrived at Le Chalet, our living room floor was covered with a light blue carpet, stained from years of wear. We pulled it out before we even brought in our first boxes. What was underneath

was to be expected. It was a subfloor that had been installed when the farmhouse was added on to. There were seams and nail holes. But despite this, I continued to push forward with my vision. I wanted to keep the subfloors exposed, in all their raw and imperfect glory, and I wanted to *paint them.*

So after the last staple had been pulled and years of filth had been vacuumed away, I did what any sane, totally normal person would do: I stayed up until the wee hours of the morning painting the floor. Other than a small area lit by a vintage lamp, the room was pitch-black. The perfect recipe for professionally painted floors, no doubt.

I've since taken my love of painted floors to new heights. The kitchen floor we ripped out exposed tongue-and-groove flooring, original to the 1909 farmhouse. How could I possibly cover that texture and history with new flooring? I painted it, and then stenciled it, to highlight its incredible imperfections.

Spring has since become the time on the farm for us to move all of the furniture out of the rooms to freshen them up. One of the perks of painted floors is how easy they are! Roll on the paint, let it dry, and move all the furniture back into place for an instant facelift.

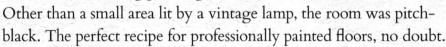

MY FAVORITE SHADES FOR FLOORS

Off-white. Allows colored furniture, vintage rugs, and the details of a room to shine.

Gray. No matter the shade, gray has a soothing vibe to it and also brings a gentle warmth to a space.

Yellow. There's something about a bold, rich yellow that makes me so very happy! It's comfortable, warm, and inviting.

THE COLORS OF SPRING

When I was a florist, my mentor encouraged me to stick with a palette of three focal colors in any arrangement. This was helpful in learning how to design a room, though admittedly, it still took me time to layer the colors correctly. And maybe I still don't (but at least I understand the concept).

In the first house Stuart and I lived in, each wall was a different color. The busyness drove me mad! So to counter the chaos, I utilized the only color palette I was comfortable with at the time: brown and green. I know, I know—not the best design decision I've ever made . . .

Regardless of how I tried to venture out (I did paint a bathroom navy blue once), I always came back to "beige-land," as my dearest friend Angela calls it. When I began studying English and French cottage design, I found interiors that were filled with shades of burgundy, red, black, blue, and gold. I no longer feared color; instead I layered it with confidence.

For spring, I find the richness of greens, browns, yellows, and other muted tones to be intoxicating. Rather than constantly

change out my palette from season to season (who has time for that?), I simply work in a few of these delicious seasonal colors that bring a bit of freshness to any space. Throw pillows and blankets, branches and flowers, potted plants, stacked books, table linens, and wreaths are easy ways to work them in.

Spring Celebrations

Tell the truth, work hard, and come to dinner on time.
—*GERALD R. FORD*

We're blessed to live a long stone's throw from my parents' house. Often we will herd the children into the car, only to show up at their doorstep six minutes later with hungry bellies and hearts. My mom will immediately fling open her cupboards to figure out what she can magically whip up for six more mouths. Luckily, she's had years of practice cooking for me and my two sisters, and a slew of friends and neighbors who found their way to the family table over the years. I will pour us deep glasses of wine and offload the day's events while she caramelizes onions and chops up asparagus.

My mom was the person who taught me how to set a table and set the stage for having company. There are a few rules that are so deeply ingrained in my homemaking skills, it's nearly impossible to shake them. Not that I've wanted to. My mother's table was always one of excess and comfortable style, and I was happy to bring that to my own.

For starters, bowls and plates should always be filled. Really, *really* filled. Basically, this requires the cook to double what she might normally prepare. If strawberries are to be served with whipped cream for dessert, it better be a big, ol' mess of them, dripping over the edges of the bowl and piled high in the middle. A far cry from the perfectly structured vegetable plates available at the supermarket, mom's homemade versions are always overflowing with a variety of colors and textures. The dip is scooped into a fancy bowl and is continually fluffed up by the spoon so it looks fresh and appetizing.

My mother is also insistent that there be *at least* three things served. Soup, bread, and salad. Meat, rice, and vegetables. Sandwiches, chips, and pickles. Most often, we watch Mom cook, nibble on chunks of aged cheddar, and talk about farm projects we're working through. The space is then cleared to make room for the main meal. Bowls of seasonal fruits and vegetables are strewn about, more cheeses are put out on cutting boards, olives are dumped from their glass jars into prettier dishes, more wine is poured, bread is sliced and buttered, and we begin to feast. It's not fancy food, but fresh garden and orchard produce, homemade bread, and home-raised meat that are hard to beat. It's simple, yet perfectly orchestrated, to provide the diner with a variety of colors, textures, and tastes.

Though this abundant entertaining certainly accounts for more time in the kitchen (and no doubt a slightly larger grocery bill), it also lays the foundation for keeping a home and table that is always welcoming to the passerby. The loner. The newly widowed grandparent. The hungry daughter and son-in-law with four babies who desperately need to not cook supper tonight.

My mother's table, decorated with food rather than flowers, says, *Welcome. Sit and be filled!*

At my home, I like to make sure that my guests leave with bursting waistlines and spirits by offering them the very best of what we have to offer. And spring is certainly a time when that can easily be done.

BUILDING A BEAUTIFUL SPRING TABLE

The point of the spring table is to gently bring forth what the earth is bearing, be it branches, blossoms, or early fruits. To celebrate spring on the farm, all we have to do is participate in the magic that is stirring around us!

More often than not, my family doesn't gather around a decked-out table. Most days, it's the six of us filling our bellies around a large, slightly dirty table, which is usually adorned with a jar of whatever flower or greenery is growing in the garden, a marble lazy Susan that holds our flatware (easily in the reach of little hands so they can practice their independence), and whatever tablecloth happens to be clean that day. I keep an entire collection of thrift-store tablecloths on hand. They're stained, torn, and a little tattered, but they're also ridiculously charming and fitting for the magic of the everyday ordinary.

Like me, you must learn to trust your own vision for your home. What elements do you love? What textiles make you swoon? What table settings make you enjoy your food all the more? For years, I worked under an incredible designer whose keen eye always left me nervous to give it a go myself. But I eventually realized that all it takes is a bit of confidence in a style that you already love.

Though most meals are enjoyed with humble table decor, sometimes the table calls for something a bit more extravagant. Perhaps it's your year to host an Easter brunch or a special birthday. Regardless, let's deck out our spring table—because this is how life gets beautiful.

Some things to think about:

Fabric. Every table benefits from some kind of textile. New, old, smooth, textured, ruffled, sleek, napkins, tablecloth, etc.

Cutlery. I love collecting handfuls of vintage forks and spoons every time I visit a secondhand store. None of mine match, and they're certainly never polished, but they always look perfect in jars on the table.

Plates and glasses. I'm keen on the idea that tables should be set. It is so enjoyable to carry supper out from the kitchen and place it in the center of the table. It's part of the theatrics and part of the fun! Having plates and glasses set on the table indicates purpose, intention, and a welcoming invitation. I couldn't care less if the plates and glasses are matching. Rather, I almost insist they aren't.

Life. "Life" can come in many forms on the table. Fresh flowers, bowls of fruit, potted herbs, flickering candles, even a jar of broccoli flowers or curly kale will do the trick. The point is simply to bring an element to the table that is *alive*.

Layers. The best tables have a few surprises. This could be mossy branches, grapes for nibbling, fancy labels for the cheeses, a few extra wine bottles, or small decorative additions. Bring something in that's a bit unexpected and layer it on!

Charm. When I'm serving a special supper, even if it's just for my family, I make it a point to *add charm*. For example, cheese isn't served in its store packaging. Instead, it's taken out and placed on an old wood cutting board or a piece of brown butcher paper. The same element, presented in a slightly different way, can make a massive difference in how you feel when you interact with it.

I often pair new and shiny pieces with old and well-loved ones. Just like cooking a meal, design loves contrast, which can come in the form of texture, color, or even placement. Soft, vintage fabric is strewn on the dining room table, twisted and fluffed up for texture and depth and paired with silk magnolia branches that are tangled up in the fabric to add drama. Place settings are put out, along with glasses and mason jars holding silverware. Lastly, single blossoms are added to more mason jars and placed around the table. It's a gathering of beauty, further highlighted by delicious food and drink served to those you love.

SPRING CHAOS

If you could see my house in the spring, you'd undoubtedly feel better about your own. That is assuming, of course, that you can see your floor through a layer of dirt, manure, and straw that keeps finding its way inside, often clung to my children's clothing and boots. It's also assuming that you, at some point in history, have actually done some laundry or washed a dish.

In the spring, it would seem I haven't.

It's as if the end of the winter season came and whisked Organization off for a romantic weekend, leaving behind only you-know-who: Spring Chaos.

During winter, we aren't given the choice. When you're housebound, it's easy to keep up with the dishes, laundry, housekeeping, and general tidiness (my physical appearance included). But in the spring, I'm naturally going to choose digging around in the manure pile, planting Johnny Jump Ups, trimming back lavender plants, and building herb gardens over mopping floors. Was there ever a contest? The answer is no. Obviously.

I always shudder when people visit the farm in the early spring. "Oh hey, friends," I want to tell them. "Welcome. Do you remember my friend, Spring Chaos? She's here for a visit. She made sure the kids were extra dirty today. Yes, they're still in their pajamas. No, they haven't had a bath, or lunch, or can't remember the last time they brushed their teeth. They've strewn their clothes all around their bedrooms, but instead of forcing them to clean up, Spring Chaos just kicked them outside to play in the mud and make a mess of our yard. Also, Spring Chaos wanted me to remind y'all that I didn't make any dinner for you, which means we'll most likely be eating eggs again for supper while you're here. Spring Chaos was insistent that I move manure piles and water the geraniums in the sunshine today.

My legs will ache from shoveling gravel, manure, old garden bedding, and new dirt. But Spring Chaos will insist that this ol' bag of bones presses on. Forget about eating . . . forget about obligations . . . forget about your body's needs . . . This is spring, baby. And, particularly on this farm, it takes no prisoners.

THE JOY OF SUMMER

 Live in the sunshine. Swim in the sea. Drink in the wild air.
—*RALPH WALDO EMERSON*

Summertime, the time of plenty, is certainly a season that's welcome around the farm. Summer, in many ways, gives us permission to be as busy or as lazy as we'd like. We can certainly fill our days with harvesting vegetables in the potager, weeding, cleaning, and preserving, but the days can also be just as easily filled with picnics, playtime, lazily lounging by the pond, taking long drives up into the mountains, or swimming in the river. It's the time when we get to extravagantly celebrate what the land is offering up because our hard work during the spring literally comes to fruition.

It's hard to not equate summertime with childhood. Days outside of the classroom are surely ones worth remembering. My memories include the smell of chlorine and wet cedar under a hot sun and the taste of soda and potato chips. My sisters and I would laze around until late afternoon, browning our skin and flipping through tween magazines. We could only be bothered to peel ourselves from the poolside deck to bike down to the local gas station for frozen neon-colored beverages. Obviously lots of things change when we become adults, summer schedules and dietary choices included. (Full disclosure: There are a lot fewer poolside days on our summer farm. And no neon-colored beverages are consumed.)

Summer mornings start early, often before 5:00 a.m., so that we can complete the bulk of the livestock and gardening chores before the heat of the day arrives with the rising sun. We watch it peek over the ridgeline and then anxiously race to get the milk in the fridge, gather the eggs, and fill the garden basket with the daily harvest. Because of this early rising, Stuart and I are also able to enjoy an extra espresso before the little ones wake from their slumber, which is reason enough for me to fall in love with the summer season.

The weather warms our skin and our soil and brings with it *joy*: joy for a refreshing, cold beverage after hot toil, joy for the siesta that naturally finds its way into even the busiest of days, and joy for the wild nature of the season.

To be honest, I'm quite keen on the unruliness that comes with summer. My children often strip off their clothes, leaving a trail of T-shirts and shorts behind them, to run through the fountain

sprinkler. Other times, I'll find a small flock of them and their friends hiding and playing with flowers, rocks, feathers, and vegetables in the antique metal bathtub that's kept in the potager for summer washing. Summer swim lessons consist of trips to the pond that's just a few hundred yards from our farm. Stuart and I can enjoy a midday glass of wine, which is always a good idea, while the kids float around, hunt for turtles, and swing from branches. Their hair is rarely brushed, the exception being for church on Sunday, lest anyone know what unkempt children they truly are.

Meals are often handfuls of cherry tomatoes or lemon cucumbers from the garden, rounded out with a glass of milk from our cow Cecelia, so I can at least check two food groups off the nutrition list. The children spend their days climbing the cherry trees, riding tricycles down the gravel driveway way too fast for my comfort, and hiking around a piece of the farm they've named "Nutwag" in search of dinosaur fossils and undiscovered insects. I cherish the summers they're spending on the farm while their hearts and minds are still tender enough to appreciate the magic in gathering cherries, picking green beans, and blowing dandelions.

In my world, that wonder never goes away.

MY FAVORITE PLANTS FOR POTS

Alyssum	Impatiens
Pentas	Desert rose
Daisies	Petunias
Morning glory	Cockscomb
Geraniums	Verbena
Moss rose	Bluebonnets
Grasses	Sweet potato vine
Gaillardia	Creeping Jenny
Coleus	Small trees
Bottlebrush	Hens and chicks

The Summer Garden

{ *The gardener must put some kind of twist on the existing landscape, turn its prose into something nearer poetry.*
—MICHAEL POLLAN

We certainly spend plenty of time in the summer months watering our gardens and flowers so that they, like us, can survive the summer heat. Because we live in such a warm, dry climate, it can take a lot of persistent watering to ensure the plants will live, especially if they're in pots. I've had to compost many plants that I potted with the very best of intentions, only to be beaten by the sun's rays once again. But since an array of potted plants is a key element of a summer farmhouse, I simply must continue to fight the good fight.

FOR THE LOVE OF POTTED PLANTS

A beautiful display of mismatched pots in the courtyard is worth the effort. For the biggest visual impact, I choose pots with varying textures and flowers of varying bloom times, colors, and heights.

Tips for Beautiful Pots

- Use pots with drain holes. The majority of flowers don't like to have their feet wet for too long, so having a container with drainage is important for preventing diseases and angry plants.

- When potting flowers, use a combination of high-quality organic potting mix and peat moss. The potting mix will feed the plant, and the peat moss will maintain consistent moisture levels in the pot.

- Even if your plants are in pots, they will still have the same sunlight requirements they normally would, so place your pots accordingly.

- Water consistently! For ease, this may mean putting your pots on drip lines. In the very peak of the summer, I often have to water my pots two or three times a day to keep the soil moist.

- Deadhead flowers with pruning shears after they've bloomed to keep the flowers looking good and to encourage new flowers to blossom.

TERRACOTTA

"Baked earth" pottery has been a favorite of mine since as long as I can remember. When I was eleven or twelve years old, my mom gave me full rein of a small flower garden plot that we had in our suburban backyard. I took control of that flower patch and moved in rocks, plants, and yes, terracotta pots. I won't pretend to understand how it's made, what makes it true "terracotta," or the difference between the glazes and finishes. All I know is I love it. That's reason enough for me to fill all the terracotta pots I can find with a variety of flowers, trees, and foliage.

I keep stacks of terracotta pots on hand at all times so they can age and get a nice patina (or see recipe on page 18 to create that patina yourself). Even the authentic Italian-made pots purchased from home-improvement stores are fairly inexpensive, so it's worth grabbing an armful when you have the opportunity. Terracotta pottery also works perfectly indoors, so your outdoor annuals can be brought indoors for future enjoyment once the growing season has passed.

Some things to keep in mind about terracotta:

- The traditional orange-brown terracotta is not watertight and will allow the pot to take in and expel water as necessary. If you're looking for a watertight version, opt for a glazed terracotta pot.

- Terracotta isn't just for pots! It's also commonly used to make roofing tiles. Can you imagine them on a greenhouse or shed roof? Also keep your eyes open for terracotta pavers to shape a sweet garden path or seating area.

THE POWER OF FLOWERS

I've spent many years devoted to flowers, from designing high-end floral bouquets to cultivating an array of beautiful flowers in our potager. These days, I delight in sharing my love of them with my children, who can't help but pluck off the prettiest blossoms. Each flower on our farm has been chosen for its beauty, and we revel in a rainbow of colors, smells, and bloom times. Once the black Queen of the Night tulips and violet crocuses fade, it's time for the summer flowers to come out and play. And I'll be honest—they throw a heck of a party.

Some of the first to arrive in the summer are the large, lime-green hydrangeas that fill a vast space,

resembling fireworks as they pop open. The zinnias are soon to follow and are some of my favorites. The red, pink, orange, and white blossoms quickly fill up space in the garden. Lucky for us, they'll continue to bloom until late fall. Black-eyed Susans, an eager perennial, will also begin to bloom with their dark black centers and contrasting bright yellow petals. They often self-seed in places they don't belong, and yet, for the life of me, I can't bear to pull them out. In another dozen years, the potager may resemble a wildflower haven, but I don't really mind the thought.

Besides the obvious perks of attracting birds, butterflies, bees, and other insects, flowers are a sweet reminder of the goodness of farm life. It's not all about utilitarianism. Rather, flowers remind us to appreciate the subtle beauty that surrounds us in this life. They remind us to slow down and walk through life at a steady, seasonal pace. It's physically impossible not to feel joy and peace of mind when you're walking through a flower garden (a statement I make based on my own personal research, of course). So let's plant them and plant them abundantly!

Jar Joy

Most homesteaders keep an array of jars around the home—jars for canning summer produce or even cocktails and so on. Jars are also welcome vessels for flowers. If your home is in need of instant cottage charm, grab a handful of flowers, branches, or even kale and shove them into a vintage jar. It takes almost no effort and will instantly add life and allure to any space. I learned to utilize this tactic before company came over. Didn't get the bathroom cleaned up? No problem! Throw a jar of flowers onto the counter, make sure there are no dirty diapers on the floor, and call it good.

Jars of flowers can be composed of almost any kind of vegetation. I love to throw in berry branches, grapevines, cherry tomatoes, or even radish blossoms for an unexpected surprise. No flowers? No problem. Grab some tree branches or flowering bush branches. Put on your designer hat and look around your landscape with new eyes as to what you can make use of.

As a general design rule, I try to incorporate no more than three things because I find it keeps the arrangement dramatic. For example, I might use zinnias, berry branches, and snapdragons, and lots of them! For an even more dramatic look, I might choose one flower and fill the entire jar with that alone. Vases of flowers look wonderful grouped together, so to highlight all of your favorites, vary the heights of your jars and fill each jar with a different flower. Nestle them together on a table where you'll get to enjoy them often. Flowers make a big impact when they're bunched together.

THE ART OF THE POTAGER

The European gardens and landscaping I saw on a backpacking trip through France, Italy, and Spain were the first to open my eyes to the *potager*. I was completely captivated by the walkways, moss-kissed stones, thoughtful designs, and casual comfort, and how the utilitarian rows of vegetables were softened by edges of lavender and foxglove.

I continued to fall further in love with the cottage aesthetic, both in the home and most certainly in the garden. I found myself influenced by people like Hugh Fearnley-Whittingstall, who was an English city-dweller turned homesteader. Hugh underplanted his bright purple chives with rich, red strawberries for the perfect contrast. He alternated lettuce colors and textures and created beautiful patterns in beds surrounded by tall bean trellises. He grew fruit trees in large metal planters that created a contrast of texture and color to the space.

I read once that a potager garden is best compared to a tapestry with contrasting colors, heights, textures, and elements. This is a step up from the basic backyard raised bed because the potager incorporates thoughtful design to make it as visually appealing as possible. In my garden, I employ the potager method to hide my

A huge part of the potager's charm comes from the intermingling of herbs, flowers, fruits, and vegetables. As you're planning your space, or even refreshing your beds with new plantings in the summer, incorporate a variety of all of these for maximum allure.

less-than-beautiful potato patch and chicken-nibbled beet tops. The vegetable patch is surrounded by blueberries, hollyhocks, hardy kiwi, chives, thyme, delphinium, tulips, gooseberries, roses, black-eyed Susans, coral bells, raspberries, currants, grapevines, and, of course, ridiculous amounts of lavender, so that when you approach, all you see are flowers, vines, and dramatic colors rather than the radishes that have bolted and the tomatoes that are past their prime. It's really an ingenious way for the garden to always look beautiful from the outside, even if it doesn't look great from the inside.

The traditional potager is based on geometric patterns, often created out of rock and raised beds. These small beds can be shaped and structured in any number of ways, but I'm drawn toward casual, rounded corners that are shaped by large rocks or pea gravel. If sharp, distinct lines are your thing, by all means, shape your potager beds accordingly.

A quick, hand-drawn plan will be enough to give you a bird's-eye view of your space and how it will visually look when it's all pieced together.

PAPER-WRAPPED FLOWERS

It doesn't matter how many times I make or receive them, the charm of paper-wrapped flowers continually leaves me breathless. While in Paris, my friend and I wandered the streets and gazed admiringly into the open doors of the storefronts. Vintage bikes were propped up next to paned glass windows, while intentionally placed pots of flowers dotted the sidewalk and entrance into the store. But it was the paper-wrapped flowers that spoke to my heart. They are a gift casual enough to buy for yourself, yet charming enough to give to even the fanciest of friends.

These days my paper-wrapped flowers often accompany a dozen eggs from our hens and are composed of whatever happens to be blooming in the potager that week, even if it's just herbs. Brown

craft paper happens to be my favorite, though white works just as well. Though our farm bouquets are typically wrapped with kitchen twine, beautiful ribbon is always welcome.

Cut flowers of your choice

Paper towels

Plastic wrap

Craft paper

Twine

Gather your flowers together. I love solid bunches of the same flower because of the visual impact, but use what you like!

Wet a few paper towels and squeeze them gently to remove excess water. Wrap the wet paper towels around the bottoms of the flower stems to help keep them moist. Then, wrap the wet paper towels and stems in plastic wrap.

Lay a large, square sheet of craft paper down on a flat surface and place the bunch of flowers in the middle, with the top of the flowers pointing toward a corner of the paper.

Fold one side of the paper in toward the middle, fold the bottom of the paper in, and then fold in the other side of the paper.

Lastly, using your multitasking hand skills, wrap a piece of string around the flowers and tighten.

PLAYING IN THE POTAGER'S BOUNTY

When we were still renters, I had only been gardening for a few short years before I realized just how large a bounty can come from a small vegetable patch in the summer months. Although I'd done my best to eat what was coming out of our small raised beds, I soon found myself with baskets and buckets of tomatoes, eggplants, peppers, green onions, and potatoes that were beginning to die a slow death on my kitchen counter. My aunt, who also happened to be my neighbor at the time, was kind enough to lend me her pressure canner. Perhaps being too proud to ask for help, I walked back to my house with the gigantic metal pot, wishing it had come with some sort of instruction manual. After all, I wanted to can vegetable soup with my plethora of homegrown ingredients!

Eventually, through a combination of trial and error and internet searching, I figured out how to use the pressure canner and, surprisingly, caused no major explosions in the kitchen. (I'm sure the landlord was thankful for that.) Ironically, Stuart and I didn't even eat the soup because we were both afraid I'd botched it and we'd both be poisoned by it. I've since learned how to use a pressure canner properly and make a vegetable soup that the entire family enjoys with a chunk of buttery, freshly baked bread in the winter. Victory!

The point is, of course, to celebrate the bounty of produce from the garden. This time of year, my harvest trays are filled with jewel-toned tomatoes, deep purple eggplants, a rainbow of sweet peppers, sweet ears of corn, intoxicatingly purple lavender, handfuls of bright green chives, and even the occasional artichoke. These are the days of ripe watermelon and cold beer. To quote whoever said it first, "This is as good as it gets."

Because of the unbearably hot days, I often find myself not venturing out to the potager until after the sun has just dipped below the horizon. This is a time when the farm seems calm and I can sink into the beauty that's at hand. Barefoot, I'll venture through the vegetable garden and flower patches, pulling out ripe produce and perfectly formed flowers. I have a habit of arranging the "goods" in my basket, and I'll wander back inside with this new "masterpiece" dangling from my arm. The lavender is bundled and hung to dry, eggs are transferred to the wire basket above the stove, herbs are placed in bags in the refrigerator, and the vegetables are stacked in a rustic basket on the counter. My perfectly packaged garden basket does wonders for my spirit. It's a gentle encouragement from the garden to keep cultivating beauty and a rich reminder to appreciate what's at hand.

THE PARTY IN THE GARDEN

Let's be honest here: Summer gardening is not without its drawbacks. Rest assured, bees will fly into your hair and sweat will form less-than-desirable marks on your shirt. Mulch will slip into places you never wanted it to be. Like all good parties, the summer party in the garden is a marriage of extreme fun and sweat. It's perfect.

Even for the younger members of the family who have yet to contribute, the summer garden is still *primo*. For them, the highlights are not the perfect cherry tomatoes or lima beans, but the frogs, dragonflies, and butterflies they can capture in their little nets for further investigation. Almost every rock in the garden is rolled over, at least two times per week, so that the creatures living below can be examined (the worms are always the star of the party).

The summer garden party is also the perfect time to show off your specialities. Purple pole beans, orange tomatoes, bright green eggplants, lemon cucumbers, Romanesco broccoli, and purple carrots just scratch the surface! You'd be hard-pressed to find a home gardener who didn't grow at least one novelty crop just for the fun of it. So bring out some jeweled corn at your next cookout. This is, after all, your party.

After the laborious work of the spring garden, the productive and lush summer garden is certainly a welcome spectacle. It tends to take to the lazier summer days, just like the gardener. Sure, it still requires massive amounts of weeding and tending, but if you don't get to it for a week or two . . . or a month, ahem . . . nobody cares. Instead of weeds, visitors and the gardener alike see ripe, plump fruit hanging from strong, green branches. It's easier to look beyond the bolted weeds, broken bits of planting trays, and random plastic dinosaurs that have crept into the pepper patch when there is so much bounty to be gathered! By summertime, I've lost my zeal for keeping things perfect. Frankly, I have far more pressing things to accomplish in the summer months, like cooking up tantalizing dishes and sipping mojitos.

Lest I lead you to think that summertime at Le Chalet is all about relaxation, let me shed a bit of light on how mornings work around here. Rarely is there a morning that we sleep in past 5. This far north, the sun begins to lighten the hills at around 4:30 a.m. For us, that means the rooster is crowing, the dairy cow is mooing, and the kids are soon to follow. If we wait too long, the flies will be there to greet us. Every summer morning starts with watching the sun rise up over the mountain ridge as we rhythmically milk in unison, Stuart on Cecelia's left side, me on her right.

We're often asked why we don't buy a mechanized milking machine. Summer mornings are why. There is truly no place I'd rather be in the world than tucked up under Cecelia's flank, my hands warmed by her udder, as I gently squeeze the morning milk into the bucket. Slowly, I watch the pail fill up with warm milk that always seems extra frothy on those summer mornings. I don't want this experience to be mechanized. I want to feel it. Appreciate it. Trucking back to the house with a milk bucket in one hand, an egg bucket in another, I feel richer than royalty.

I could live a lifetime of summer mornings and never tire of their offerings.

BRANCH BEAN TRELLIS

I always grow climbing beans because of the way they wind around anything they can find. Branches have been my go-to for these basic bean trellises that provide the structure climbing beans need to thrive.

Casually draw a circle in the soil, about 4 feet in diameter. Insert the branches into the soil, at least 10 inches deep, at even intervals around the circle.

8 branches, 6 feet or longer

Twine

Gather two of the branches (ones that sit opposite each other on the circumference of the circle) together in the middle. Tie them together with twine.

Gather two more branches (ones that sit opposite each other on the circumference of the circle) together in the middle of the circle along with the already-tied branches. Tie these to the branches as well with twine.

Continue gathering and tying together two branches at a time until all the branches have been bound together in the middle of the circle.

WHAT WE'RE HARVESTING
ON THE FARM

My very first garden was a summer garden, full of tomatoes, sweet peppers, corn, and herbs. I had little idea of the proper methods of growing such treats, but, to my surprise, I ended up with a surplus at the height of summer. At that time, I was still developing many of my ideas around food. So, facing a few baskets full of vegetables that I didn't know how to prepare or enjoy, I decided to do what seemed my only option: make salsa.

The irony, of course, is that I didn't know how to make salsa either. I consulted my mom's canning manual and tried my best to stay on point with the recipe. I'd never canned anything in my life, but I stirred that pot of salsa with great confidence as it simmered, proud of the harvest that had come from my small plot.

Artichokes. Say what? You can grow artichokes somewhere besides the Mediterranean? Oh yes you can! I plant a huge row each year not only because the artichokes themselves are delicious, but also because the flowers are absolutely spectacular. I let many go to flower just so I can enjoy the purple frills through the late summer. They require a long growing season, so they must be started indoors early in the spring, but it's worth the long-term commitment.

Beets. Fresh beets sliced incredibly thin on a mandolin and sprinkled with toasted, chopped almonds, chopped mint, and crumbled goat cheese is one of my summer go-to lunches. They may get a bad rap for their canned counterpart, but fresh beets (and beet greens!) in the summer garden are essential. My

garden guru encouraged me to ruthlessly thin my beet rows this year, and what a difference it made in the size of them! Lesson learned.

Corn. I grow a small patch of corn each year so that I can enjoy the stalks for decorating in the fall, but I've yet to master growing it for consistent ears for eating. Rather, I'm happy to head to the market a few times each summer to stock up on loads of it. "Hey, kids! Guess what we're having for dinner? Corn!" They don't mind.

Eggplant. Not as common as most vegetables in the summer garden, eggplant has nevertheless earned its keep in our potager. The long, purple orbs dangle from the silvery branches with such display, I can't resist growing them because they are simply magnificent.

Green beans. If there is a more romantic vegetable to harvest than the green bean, I've yet to find it. I gather up my apron to collect each bean, carefully picked one at a time, and then drop them into a nearby basket and do it again. This is one task I often keep for myself because the pleasure runs so deep.

Melons. Another garden crop that I often rely on others to grow for me, I still can't help but squeeze a few watermelon vines or cantaloupes here and there in the potager because I love the way they fill in and snake around the garden beds. That being said, the bulk of what we eat still comes from the back of pickup trucks and small roadside stands that set up each summer along our route into town. I suppose it's for the best anyway, since my chickens always seem to find a way into mine.

Okra. It wasn't until we lived in Alabama that I was able to enjoy this summer vegetable and its unique flavor. After all, okra is still an uncommon ingredient here in the Pacific Northwest. I ensure we plant it when the soil is warm enough so that we can enjoy it fried, pickled, and sautéed.

Peaches. Though I can make quite a case for the delicious taste of Washington peaches, my Georgia-born husband still clings to the notion that his state's peaches are somehow better. Though we may disagree on that, we don't disagree about our love for this luscious summer fruit. Until our peach tree grows

up to the point of production, we'll continue to enjoy them from our neighbor's organic orchard.

Peppers. Peppers like it hot, and lucky for me, we live in an area that is dry and warm enough to grow a wide variety. Each year, I fill the garden with sweet and hot peppers that will later be used every way imaginable in the kitchen. Peppers are the garden's way of welcoming us into full-fledged summer. We eat only local peppers, and only in the summertime, because this is when they're the very best. Always plant more than you think you should.

Plums. An often-understated fruit, plums still have much to offer on the summer menu. I can't resist having bowls of the plump little purple fruits sitting around. My kids enjoy them like candy, and they look quite lovely en masse.

Tomatoes. I didn't always love tomatoes. It took years to acclimate my palate to their acidic flavor and squishy insides. I once heard it said that you should try something at least seventeen times before you commit to not liking it, and frankly, I'm glad I took that advice. Now I love tomatoes roasted, simmered into sauces, mixed fresh with pasta, or even just drizzled with a bit of sweet balsamic vinegar. They are the king of the summer garden, and rightfully so.

Zucchini and summer squash. Most people tell some variation of the story that begins, "Don't leave your front door unlocked in the summer or people will drop zucchini off at your house!" It's true. There's hardly a better producer than a few zucchini plants in the garden, offering up an abundant harvest for the better part of three months before giving way to heat or squash beetles.

Summer Recipes

 Our deep respect for the land and its harvest is the legacy of generations of farmers who put food on our tables, preserved our landscape, and inspired us with a powerful work ethic.
—*JAMES H. DOUGLAS JR.*

It wouldn't be right to talk about summer food without talking about outdoor cooking. Even after a long day of work on or off the farm, it's still worth setting up the grill, cracking open a beer, and savoring the golden daylight.

Stuart will often man the grill on our homestead, mainly because I enjoy the break and don't particularly enjoy standing around the grill, fiddling with the food. He loves it. So while I gather side dishes on the table and pour glasses of rosé, he grills peppers, onions, eggplants, corn, and lamb roasts. Django Reinhardt guitar melodies float through the thick, hot air while we catch up on the day's events and the kids run wild, all of us held off from hunger by bowls of olives and cubes of cheese. There's no rush. No place to be. Our only clock is the placement of the sun in the sky, and if the night goes well, the moon.

MY FAVORITE POTATO SALAD

Much unlike the gooey and bland potato salad sold at the supermarket, proper potato salad is a vibrant and flavorful treat to behold. I'm not one for mayonnaise, so this yogurt dressing is a perfect alternative. The slightest zing of mustard is a nice contrast to the creamy potatoes.

Serves a huge summer crowd

Cut the potatoes into 1-inch pieces and combine them with the sea salt in a pot of water. Bring to a boil and simmer for 10–12 minutes, until fork-tender. Drain and transfer the potatoes to a large bowl. Set aside to cool.

In a medium-size bowl, combine the yogurt, mustard, salt, black pepper, and shallots.

Add the celery, parsley, and eggs to the bowl of potatoes. Pour the yogurt mixture over the potatoes and stir to dress the entire salad. Season to taste with salt and pepper before placing in the refrigerator.

Serve chilled with a pinch of additional parsley.

4 pounds peeled russet potatoes

½ cup sea salt

1 cup whole-fat plain yogurt

2 teaspoons grainy mustard

1½ teaspoons salt

1 teaspoon freshly ground black pepper

2 shallots, minced

1 cup minced celery

5 tablespoons minced fresh parsley

6 hard-boiled eggs, peeled and sliced

GARDEN MINT MOJITOS

I first fell in love with mint mojitos on our honeymoon, when something equally tangy and sweet seemed to hit the spot perfectly. Mint was one of the first perennials I planted on the farm, and if I were to be honest, I would confess 99 percent of it is used for this perfect summer beverage. Everyone is a bit more laid back after a garden mint mojito. **Serves 1**

2 tablespoons honey simple syrup (recipe below)

12 fresh mint leaves

2 lime wedges

Juice of ½ lime

3 ounces white rum

½ cup sparkling mineral water or club soda

Ice

In a large, sturdy glass, combine the honey simple syrup, mint leaves, and lime wedges. Use a muddler or spoon to squish the juice from the lime wedges and crush the mint, releasing its beautiful fragrance in the process.

Add the additional lime juice, rum, and mineral water. Stir to combine.

Fill the remaining space with ice and enjoy immediately. And then enjoy another.

HONEY SIMPLE SYRUP

We keep honey simple syrup on hand for all of our cocktail needs. Honey has a much more complex flavor than white sugar, and it lends itself well to mixed drinks.

Honey

Water

Combine equal parts honey and water in a small saucepan. Heat the mixture until the honey is melted and well combined with the water, stirring as needed.

Store the simple syrup in a jar in the refrigerator and use to sweeten cocktails.

GRILLED EINKORN FLATBREADS

I often knead up a double batch of these einkorn flatbreads to pair with grilled meats and vegetables. My kids will roll them into imperfect circles outside, where the messy flour can spill on the ground. The flatbreads can cook on the grill when the meat and vegetables are finished, taking just a few minutes per side to cook. They're chewy, almost pita-like, and are a wonderful tool to scoop up all the delicious food. **Serves 6**

Sift the flour into a large bowl. Add the honey, salt, yeast, and water. Stir to completely combine.

Add more flour, as needed, to get a thick-dough consistency.

Knead the dough in the bowl for 5–10 minutes. By the end of this time, the dough should be smooth.

Divide the dough into 15 pieces. On a heavily floured surface, roll each piece into a circle using a floured rolling pin. You can obtain nice, smooth edges by folding all the outer edges into the middle prior to rolling it out.

Preheat a dry cast-iron skillet on medium-high until it's smokin' hot. Alternatively, this can be done directly on a hot grill.

Add a flatbread to the skillet and cook for 1 minute, until it bubbles in the middle. Flip it over and cook for 1 more minute. Repeat with the remaining flatbreads.

Brush the flatbreads with melted butter and give them a sprinkle of garlic salt. Divine!

4 cups all-purpose einkorn flour

2 tablespoons honey

3 teaspoons salt

3½ teaspoons yeast

1½ cups warm water

Melted butter, for serving

Garlic salt, for serving

SUMMER QUICHE

When vegetables and eggs are coming in by the basketful, it's prime time for making up this summer quiche. Use whatever vegetables you have on hand. Corn and peppers is my favorite summer combination. **Serves 8**

1⅓ cups all-purpose flour (einkorn is my favorite)

½ teaspoon sea salt

½ cup butter, chilled

9 eggs

1 tablespoon butter

2 small yellow onions, minced

3 medium sweet peppers, seeded and chopped

Corn from 1 cob, about 1 cup

1 cup heavy cream

4 ounces cream cheese (optional)

1 cup grated aged cheddar

Large pinch of sea salt

2 tablespoons minced parsley

In a stand mixer with the paddle attachment, combine the flour and ½ teaspoon salt. Cube the ½ cup of chilled butter into small pieces and drop them in, a few at a time, while the mixer is on medium-low speed. Once the flour mixture begins to resemble coarse sand, add 1 egg and mix to combine.

Remove the dough from the mixer, wrap it in plastic wrap, and stick it in the fridge for at least 30 minutes to chill. The dough can also be made ahead of time and kept in the fridge for up to 3 days.

When ready to bake the quiche, remove the dough from the refrigerator and flour a work surface. Use a rolling pin, and additional flour as needed, to roll the dough into a 12-inch round.

Line a 9-inch springform cake pan with aluminum foil. Gently lift the dough round and place it over the cake pan, using your fingertips to gently press the dough into the pan. Use any excess hanging over the sides to patch holes, if needed. Make sure there aren't cracks or holes—this will be holding a liquid substance! And unless you want to scrape burnt egg out of your oven (lame), I suggest you make sure that crust is watertight, baby.

Put the crust in the fridge until needed. Preheat the oven to 375°F.

Heat a small skillet over medium-high heat and melt 1 tablespoon of butter. Add the minced onion, chopped peppers, and corn. Sauté for 4–6 minutes, until soft. Turn off the heat and set the veggies aside.

In your stand mixer, combine the remaining 8 eggs, cream, cream cheese, cheddar cheese, and a pinch of sea salt. Mix until completely combined. Then, add the sautéed vegetables and parsley. Mix until just combined.

Remove the crust from the refrigerator, pour in the egg mixture, and bake for 40–45 minutes, until lightly golden on the top and the quiche has just the slightest jiggle in the center.

Remove the quiche from the oven and let it sit for a few minutes before removing the springform pan. Allow it to sit for just a minute or two more before slicing.

QUICK PICO DE GALLO

I mix up a pico de gallo, or salsa fresca, almost every day during the peak of the summer. It's a quick, fresh salsa that is beautiful on top of all varieties of meat. If meat isn't on the menu, simply use it as a dip for tortilla chips. With its bright and acidic flavor, it's wonderfully refreshing. **Serves 6**

Combine the cabbage, peppers, onion, tomatoes, and cilantro in a large bowl.

In a small bowl, whisk together the lime juice, sea salt, pepper, and vinegar.

Pour the vinegar mixture over the cabbage mixture and stir to incorporate. Season to taste with salt and pepper.

I like to let my pico de gallo sit for about an hour before eating it so the flavors can marry a bit, but it's certainly not necessary. Refrigerate the pico de gallo until you're ready to serve it.

½ medium-size head of cabbage, cored and sliced extremely thin

3 sweet peppers, seeded and diced

1 small onion, minced

2 tomatoes, seeded and diced

½ cup chopped cilantro

Zest and juice of 1 lime

Large pinch of sea salt

½ teaspoon freshly ground black pepper

4 tablespoons raw apple cider vinegar

CARAMELIZED PEACHES

These caramelized peaches were so good the first time I made them, I had to do it again to *make sure* they were as awesome as I thought they were. I invited my parents over to share in this peachy goodness. They moaned while they were eating them, so I guess they were, in fact, as good as I thought. Unless they just felt like moaning randomly at supper . . . and that's just too weird, so I'll assume that wasn't the case. **Serves 6**

8 large, very ripe peaches

½ cup butter

1 cup dehydrated whole cane sugar

1 cup cream

Pinch of sea salt

2 tablespoons chopped mint

2 tablespoons chopped almonds

Peel the peaches, cut them in half, and remove the pits. Set aside.

Melt the butter, cane sugar, cream, and a pinch of salt in a pan. Heat the mixture over low heat and allow the butter to melt and meld with the sugar and cream. Stir it gently. Alternatively, this can easily be done in a cast-iron skillet over a hot grill outdoors.

Continue heating the mixture for 5 minutes, until it starts to look like caramel. No need to stir it—just keep an eye on it. You don't want your caramel to burn; however, you must give it time to caramelize. Smell it. Taste it. Once it's hit the magic point and is the consistency and smell of caramel, add the peaches.

Allow the peaches to heat up in the caramel for 3 minutes. Flip them over and give them 3 more minutes.

Once the peaches are heated through, remove the skillet from the heat. Top the peaches with the mint and almonds and a dash of cream, if you so desire. Serve immediately.

GIN AND GRAPEFRUIT

After a day out in the summer heat, pulling weeds or harvesting in the garden, Stuart often greets me with a cocktail. He's the resident cocktail maker around these parts, and I'm more than happy to oblige him with the title. Sometimes it's in a fancy glass with citrus zest or a sprig of rosemary, but more often, it's in a mason jar. When the heat of the day has eased and we're able to sit in the courtyard and slowly sip our gin and grapefruit, it feels like we'll be able to patch up the messy world around us. "We'll get 'em tomorrow," we say. But for now, we sip and savor. **Serves 1**

In a cocktail shaker, combine the gin, grapefruit juice, maple syrup, and enough ice to fill the shaker. Put the top on and shake vigorously for 15 seconds.

Pop the top off and pour the mixture into a chilled glass. Add the sparkling wine and enough ice to fill the glass. Garnish with a sprig of rosemary.

2 ounces gin

4 ounces freshly squeezed grapefruit juice

1 teaspoon maple syrup, or to taste

Ice

Splash of sparkling wine

Sprig of rosemary, for garnish

Summer in the Home

While the magic of the summer may be primarily happening out in the fields and gardens, the inside of the summer farmhouse should certainly not be forgotten. The home will serve as a cool retreat from the brutal heat and after a dirty, laborious day. I often take a cool shower to wash away the dirt of the day, curl up on the couch, and pray someone will show up to wash the dishes. This doesn't usually happen, but I'm able to relax nonetheless, because the house is designed for just that.

When I'm feeling most inspired outdoors, which is during the summertime, I'm often feeling most inspired indoors. That presents a major problem! What's a farmgirl to do when she's entrenched in summer weeding *and* imagining how good the stairs would look with a runner and additional potted houseplants?

Just this past summer, right when my counters were heavy with bins of red tomatoes and spicy peppers, baskets of eggplant, bags of basil, and bowls of berries, I decided it'd be the perfect time to move an area rug into the dining room. "Don't do it," Stuart warned.

"It's not the time for that." Oh, but surely it was! After all, I could picture the display in all its glory. The tattered red rug would lie under the antique pie cabinet, which is currently home to a variety of drink glasses and cookbooks. I would move the orchid from the living room to the top of the cabinet and use a few odds and ends to highlight the photographs of babies and Paris that surround it. I'd hang vintage aprons and a few braids of onions to the left of the cabinet. It would be beautiful! I simply couldn't resist (and thankfully, he was willing to help after all).

I wouldn't say that summer is the perfect time to move your creative energy indoors. After all, there is still plenty of farm work to do. However, it's worth it to make sure the home feels right for the season. This is done by incorporating seasonal elements, like flowers and fruit, and keeping the space light and relaxing with soft textiles and bright colors. At this time of year, you won't find coats hanging on the pegs in the kitchen, heavy blankets laid over the arms of the sofa, or firewood stacked by the fireplaces. Even the majority of our throw pillows have been moved outside, where the kids spend the warm mornings reading, crafting, and making messes in their tent.

SUMMER TEXTILES

Do you feel like curling up by the fire with a heavy, wool blanket come July? Certainly not! So why have that blanket draped over the arm of the couch? It's time to box that baby up and bring out fabrics that are breezy, light, and comfortable. Around these parts, that means cotton is king.

> **Cotton.** Cotton is a light and fluffy fabric that is breathable. The way in which it is woven allows air to freely flow in and out. This is why summer dresses are often made of cotton, as are T-shirts and tank tops. Incorporate cotton into your home by using lightweight cotton blankets on beds and couches.

Fringe. I'm a sucker for *anything* with a fringe. It keeps the vibe relaxed and playful. Incorporate fringe on pillows, throw blankets, and even tablecloths for an extra textural element.

Lace. Perhaps it's the surge of weddings that occur in the summer, but I can hardly think about the season's wardrobe without thinking of lace. Although I don't often wear lace myself (perhaps it's a farmgirl thing), I do love decorating with it indoors. During the summer, my kitchen windows are decorated with vintage lace curtains that I snagged for cheap on Etsy. It keeps the sunlight just slightly at bay, while allowing the light to still brighten the room. I'm all about the texture, and lace has it!

Cotton clothes often shrink in the dryer, making them the perfect textile to hang from your outdoor clothesline instead. Allow the summer heat to save you some energy and make your clothes smell better all at once!

Silk. Another breathable summer fabric, silk is lightweight and capable of holding up to the summer heat. Though more often worn than woven into blankets, silk is an airy accompaniment to any occasion whether in the form of a dress, skirt, or sheets. I save my silk tops for visits to the winery, when the likelihood of getting garden soil or chicken manure on them is rare.

White sheets. Whether you need a picnic blanket or a screen for your movie projector, white sheets will serve you well in the summer months. They can be spread out and tied to tree branches for a quick bit of shade or laid over the couches so dirty little kiddos can nap without soiling the sofa. I even use them as tablecloths on my makeshift tables! They're inexpensive and easily washed for use again and again and again . . .

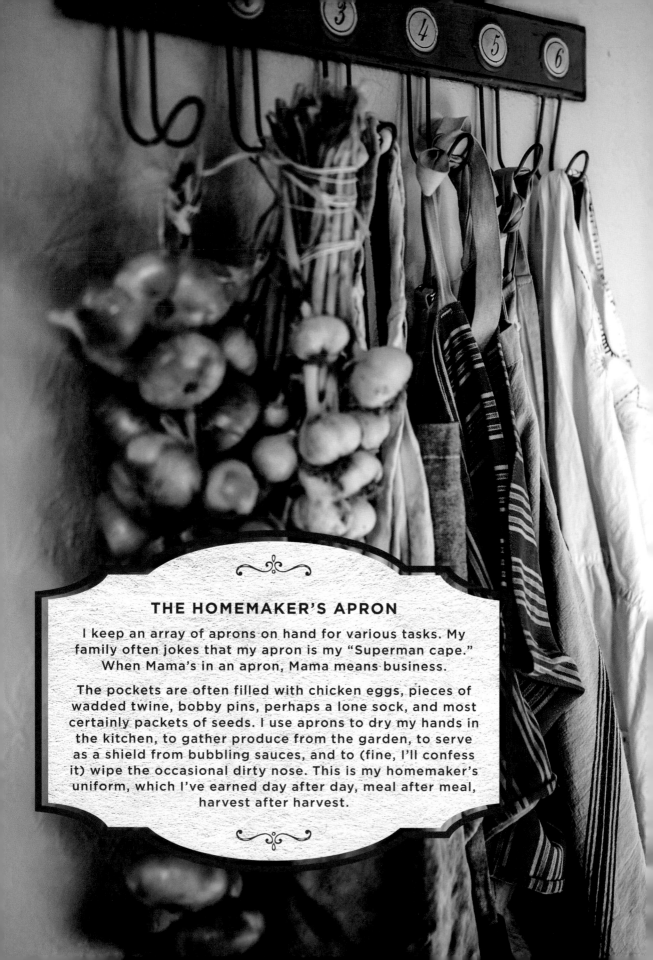

THE HOMEMAKER'S APRON

I keep an array of aprons on hand for various tasks. My family often jokes that my apron is my "Superman cape." When Mama's in an apron, Mama means business.

The pockets are often filled with chicken eggs, pieces of wadded twine, bobby pins, perhaps a lone sock, and most certainly packets of seeds. I use aprons to dry my hands in the kitchen, to gather produce from the garden, to serve as a shield from bubbling sauces, and to (fine, I'll confess it) wipe the occasional dirty nose. This is my homemaker's uniform, which I've earned day after day, meal after meal, harvest after harvest.

COTTAGE ELEMENTS FOR SUMMER

Given a choice of hobbies, I would surely put antiquing (or "thrifting") at the top of my list, and I'm sure
I'm not alone! To decorate a cottage is to fill it with
all manner of knickknacks. These items can be inspi-
rational, vintage, and charmingly rustic. Summer
is often the time for yard sales and outdoor antiques
shows. If you're in the market for items covered in
chipped paint and rust, this is your season! Plan to
attend local events with a companion and a pickup
truck so you have plenty of strength and room to get
the items where they belong: your farmhouse.

DISTRESSING PAINT TECHNIQUE

I've distressed almost every thrift-store furniture find I've ever
brought home. Though it may sound quite odd, I often find that
thrift items *speak to me*. Obviously, not literally . . . but almost. As I
browse the booths, I focus on the items in front of me. I find myself
drawn to items that are authentically old and worn. New distressed
items don't quite hit the spot for me. And yes, I can almost always
tell the difference.

"Better, not more" is the shopping mantra I use, and it's served
me well. That being said, there are a few items that I regularly pick
up, such as baskets, copper anything, flower pots, vintage aprons,
and old books, regardless of whether there is a real *need* for them.
My daughter once brought me a broken pitchfork as a gift. I chuck-
led before saying, "Well, thank you! Why did you decide to give
this to me?" She smiled and responded, "Because you love old broken things!" From the mouth of babes . . .

If you can't quite find the old piece you're looking for, have no
fear! There are methods of creating that beautiful, aged patina that
makes a piece *feel* old. I don't know if it's a technique as much as

an art form. The point is to replicate wear and tear where the item would naturally show it. For example, chairs will often wear on the bottoms of their feet and legs, and on the top of their arms and backs. As you learn to develop your distressing technique, it's valuable to take note of such things so that you can create a piece that is convincingly old. My favorite method calls for antiquing wax.

Paint color of choice

Dark or light antiquing wax

Cheap paint brushes

Washcloth

Paint the item with your paint color of choice. I always use inexpensive paint brushes to give a slightly rough, imperfect color base to start with. If your piece is already a color you like, skip this step. If not, allow the paint to dry completely.

Dip another dry paintbrush into the antiquing wax. Begin to spread the wax over the edges and unique embellishments of the piece. Dirt and grime would naturally collect in the corners and cracks, which is why we'll start there first. Our darkest wax should be in these areas.

Without putting more wax on your brush, begin to use a variety of paint strokes to spread the wax around. A little goes a long way, so take your time to massage it into the piece, concentrating on keeping it imperfect and inconsistent. Concentrate on a small section at a time.

When a section is done to your liking, gently buff it out a bit with a clean, dry washcloth. This will help soften the edges of the brush lines and allow you to wipe off any excess wax.

BEADED CHIMES

Sometimes on a summer afternoon, we like to combine my love of old things with my daughter's love of crafting. Making beaded chimes is a fun way to do this.

Insert as many eye hooks as you'd like in a straight line down one side of the branch.

String the beads, bells, and shiny things onto strips of wire and attach each beaded strand to an eye hook. You can alternate lengths of wire or keep them all the same, whatever looks best to you.

Insert two more eye hooks at opposite ends of the branch and put a piece of wire between them to create a hanging loop for the chime.

Hang the chime in the kitchen window, where it will catch the sunlight, and relax with the lazy flow of the season.

Small eye hooks

1 small branch (2 inches in diameter and about 12 inches long)

Variety of beads, buttons, bells, and shiny things (old or new)

Lightweight, pliable wire

THE COLORS OF SUMMER

I've already confessed that I was stuck in a green and brown phase for the better part of five years, but thankfully that phase passed. I found ways to incorporate shades that I was naturally drawn to, such as mustard yellows, blacks, deep reds, bright orange, golds, and French blue. My love for vibrant emerald green still lives on, but it's now been incorporated with other farmhouse shades to create a balance of colors that brings depth to the space.

I tend to steer clear of "matchy-matchy" color schemes and opt instead for colors that work well together. You won't find a blue living room or a green and white bathroom in our cottage. Rather, you'll see a rainbow of colors that mix and match with ease. Our goal for summer is to create an indoor space that is reflective of the rich and abundant season around us. For color palettes, this means we can fearlessly incorporate vibrant, saturated shades.

By all means, find colors that bring you peace. If blue and yellow make you tense, don't use them together! Color is power and can greatly affect your mood, so find ones that visually bring you satisfaction.

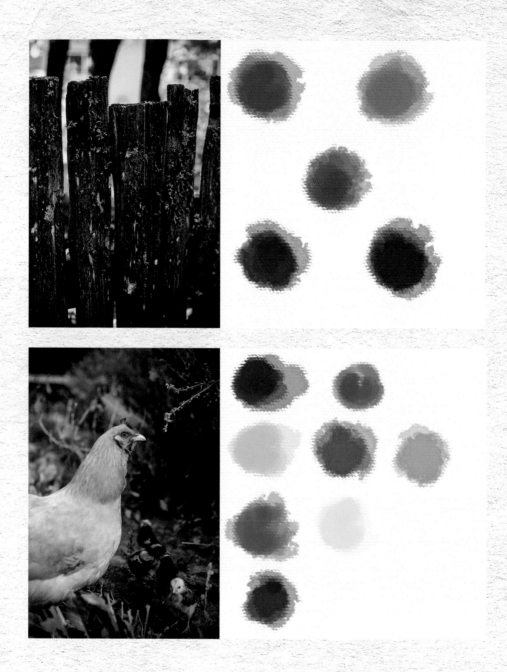

I always keep a bucket and small roller brush in the basement for quick painting sessions, freshening up walls and corners that take the most wear and tear. It's a great way to refresh the space and cover up dings, scrapes, and marker drawings. Simply wrap the roller in wet paper towels and plastic wrap between painting sessions to keep it moist.

The Perfect Neutral Background Shade

Before we moved to Le Chalet, the interior walls were slathered in varying shades of creams, mints, and yellows. Needless to say, repainting was an absolute must. In the weeks leading up to our move-in date, I consulted a variety of magazines to find the perfect shade for the walls that would serve as a canvas for all of our future design choices.

I am eternally thankful to my dear friend Angela and her husband Joel (who happens to be a professional painter) for recommending the paint that I ended up using. "You *have* to use this paint," Angela explained. "It's like concrete meets neutral meets depth" (or something to that effect). I told her I'd give it a try.

All it took was seeing the color on the paint chip for me to fall deeply in love with it, so I bought ten gallons. I imagine this is the sort of color you'd find on the walls of an old castle. The walls in our home are almost exclusively made of stucco, and the paint's muted gray highlights their texture in the most flattering way. Now every wall in our home is painted this color—ceilings included.

Summer Celebrations

It was June, and the world smelled of roses. The sunshine was like powdered gold over the grassy hillside.
—MAUD HART LOVELACE

Summer's long, drawn-out days afford us extra time for sipping mojitos, nibbling bite-size food, and celebrating with friends. It's quite possibly the easiest season in which to entertain, as extra meat can always be thrown on the grill and another lemonade poured for last-minute company.

On the farm, summertime entertaining naturally follows a common theme: work. When there are many berries to be harvested, many weeds to be pulled, or a large project that needs extra hands, it's common to invite friends and neighbors over to assist in the process. This past summer I traded a supper of roasted chicken for laying flagstone and Parisian gnocchi for help seeding the pasture. Not a bad trade, is it? Our friends contribute a few hours of sweaty, manual labor on the farm and are paid in overfilled plates and cups. Luckily, I still have quite a few takers when I ask, so perhaps the payout is worth the cost of admission.

When my sisters and I were young, summertime celebrations revolved much less around manual labor and much more around a grill in the backyard, as many American homes do. Some form of mystery meat was tossed onto the charcoal, and we were given a few more minutes to ride our bikes around the neighborhood, leaving our parents to enjoy their adult lemonade in peace. We would come back ready to devour the banquet of meats in all their grilled glory. Plates were filled with the foods familiar at our backyard summer parties: a potato dish of some sort, chips, watermelon slices, and pasta salad. For the kids and grownups alike, it was utterly delightful.

My family was never one for over-the-top summer entertainment, opting instead for games we could easily play in our backyard, such as croquet. When the sun began to fade, the party often moved inside to the kitchen table, where intense card games ensued. The sound of a shuffling deck still leaves me with excited anticipation.

Unfortunately, my children are a little too young to be taught poker. For now, we continue to entertain in the summer with grilled meats (though they're hardly a mystery anymore) and an array of whatever the garden is growing. Most of the time, my apron is a little less than clean and the entire family is barefoot. A last-minute bouquet of zinnias might decorate whatever table we're eating off of, even if it's just the tailgate of a pickup truck. You see, there are no qualifications for good summer entertaining. It could just as easily be a bottle of beer and tacos over a game of Texas Hold 'Em as an elaborately decorated feast of eggplant parmesan.

I think the point of summer entertaining is twofold: to enjoy the bounty of the season and to celebrate that bounty with others. When fruit is plucked from the trees, berries are harvested from the bushes, and an array of vegetables can be pulled from the garden, it makes entertaining all the more spontaneous and fun.

OUTDOOR DINING

Though meals can easily be enjoyed in a variety of settings, there is something distinctly special about a meal enjoyed outdoors during the summertime. After all, the air smells of honeysuckle! These moments allow us to pause during the day, and often they turn into elongated breaks, as you take a bit longer than usual to sip your morning coffee. In the summer, it's worth pretending there aren't pressing matters to attend to.

One of the great joys of the human experience is the one that comes with sharing a meal. What is it about this act that's so comforting? So lovely? So uplifting? It's as if food was created to share with others. In that spirit, the summer table becomes a celebration of fellowship as it fills up with neighbors, friends, grandkids, coworkers, and family. No longer bound by the confines of indoor seating, the summer table sets the stage for community and one of the fundamental cornerstones of the human experience: the breaking of bread. This is all the more reason to make it uniquely special, whether it's rustic, casual, or even slightly formal.

Makeshift Tables

When Stuart and I were newlyweds, we moved to the Deep South for a spell. It was a big transition for me, but I found a beautiful community of people who made our adventure one of the most special times I've ever experienced.

A local farmer named Chip met with me each week to fill my van with foods I could only have ever dreamed of. Grapefruits that took two hands to hold. Satsuma oranges. Sweet potatoes, cabbages, pecans, peanuts, and fresh lemons. Our grocery budget that year was $40 a week, but because of Chip's amazing yet inexpensive produce, we were able to stay well fed.

We didn't often share our table with others that year, but for Stuart's birthday we decided to celebrate and throw caution (and budget) to the wind. We cooked up a "low country boil," an enormous pot filled with corn, potatoes, and crawfish. There were so many pots that we had to find some makeshift tables. Luckily, we had a few hay bales, some old pieces of wood, and an old door.

And thus began my love affair with pop-up outdoor eating spaces.

An old door on hay bales is not only charming as a table, but it works well, too! Extra hay bales can also be used as chairs with small blankets or thick sheets laid on top to keep folks from getting poked in the backside.

Likewise, sawhorses can work just as well. An old piece of plywood can be used as the surface of the table. Simply add a tablecloth to dress it up and hide the less-than-charming plywood.

In orchard country where we live now, large wooden apple bins can often be found for free on the side of the road. Flip them over so that the bottom is on the top, and it's a perfectly rustic makeshift table.

OUTDOOR LIGHTING

I think there's a reason people love to sit around a fire. Maybe it's because the glow from the flames makes the world look stunning! Outdoor lighting in the summer works very much the same way, though it's much less of a fire hazard. Flames are a no-go when the hills are dry and the weather is warm. It's easy to replace the ambiance of a fire with the gentle glow of any of the following outdoor lights, which can transform an outdoor space into something enchanted.

If you're installing string lights that span 12 feet or more, it's helpful to install a "guide wire" that the string lights can be wrapped around to provide additional strength and structure.

String lights. Ideal to hang over a casual outdoor eating space, string lights can be draped and strung up just about anywhere—tree branches, pergolas, garden arches, etc. Make sure to purchase ones for outdoor use, as they will withstand the elements much better.

Electric lanterns. These can be used to light up a table, work space, or outdoor bar area and can easily be carried around if the party moves elsewhere.

Pendant lights. The more permanent option, a pendant light is often hardwired, though it can plug in to an extension cord. A pendant light is best used over a permanent outdoor area, such as a pergola.

Bamboo Shade Cover

Just like a makeshift table, a makeshift shade is also sometimes a necessity for outdoor eating. In this case, it's to block the harsh rays of the sun. My go-to is always bamboo shade covers. They can be picked up from any local home-improvement store and

are fairly inexpensive (about $75 for a 9-by-7-foot sheet). They're light enough to be strung up or hung over any assortment of poles, trees, or combination thereof. Bamboo shade covers have a unique French-country feel about them (that, quite frankly, I am crazy about) and are much more cottagey than an umbrella. We even keep a few pieces permanently above our kitchen entrance, which are now wonderfully intertwined with wisteria.

FOOD ON THE GO

What is it about food on the go that makes it so special? A sandwich eaten at your supper table doesn't taste the same as one eaten by the river. Although eating by the river isn't always possible,

Jazz up your picnic with cool, sparkling mineral water. It'll quench your thirst, replenish any minerals you've lost from perspiring, and look beautiful in a champagne glass or mason jar with a fresh fruit garnish. It's the perfect beverage to sip while you wait for the appropriate time to pour the real deal.

SUMMER PICNIC MENUS

Menu #1: Summer quiche, simple green salad with vinaigrette, sliced peaches, pickles, and kombucha

Menu #2: Meat from a roasted chicken, pasta salad, grapes, mixed nuts, and lemonade

Menu #3: Ham and butter baguette sandwiches, potato salad, olives, berries and honey, and sparkling mineral water with lemon slices

summer is the season when it happens more often than not. Even if it means just eating on a bench in the flower garden or on the tailgate of your pickup truck, it's worth packing up your food and taking it to go.

We live a short walk from a large pond that's used to irrigate the orchards that surround our farm. The pond is home to a variety of creatures that many little farmhands find fascinating. My children in particular can often be found wading in the water. They'll take a break only at the promise of food, be it sandwiches, baked goods, or fruit. I almost always sneak a bottle of wine into the picnic basket when we head to the pond. As my eyes take in the colorful scenery, my stress begins to melt away, and there is cause for celebration. Cheers to summertime.

DIY BEER BARROW

When finger foods are at hand, drinks should never be far away, and it's certainly easy to incorporate a beer barrow (that is, a wheelbarrow filled with ice and drinks). Drink tables are always welcome, but a beer barrow is also a charming way to display drinks on ice to guests and allows them to add their own offering to the stash. Sparkling water, microbrews, kombucha, and bottled lemonade are a few of our personal favorites.

Finger Foods

Outdoor cooking on the farm often revolves around food that's easily eaten with our hands. After all, we're given five senses and incorporating *touch* into our mealtime is a way to deepen the enjoyment. Part of the appeal of kebabs, tacos, or sandwiches is that they're consumed in one hand with a drink in the other. Pleasure is never more than a small arm movement away.

The farm provides us with many finger foods. Cherry tomatoes, cucumber slices, green beans, berries, melon slices, deviled

TABLE DECOR

There are effortless ways to bring cottage charm to your eating spaces and remind your guests that while summer is casual and comfortable, it's most certainly still a celebration.

Empty wine bottles filled with flowers

Vegetable displays

Potted plants

Tree branches

Terracotta pots

eggs, pickled peppers, new potatoes, cheese curds, and nuts are just a few delicious examples of food that tastes better licked from your fingers. Incorporating finger foods into your outdoor dining experience ensures that your guests will spend plenty of time lingering around the table. Summertime, after all, is about such things.

SUMMER BOUNTY

Summer on the farm is a time of extremes. The sun, the fun, the work, the harvest, and the weeds all culminate in a few short months. The fun that takes place in the summertime is enough to carry us through even the bleakest of winters. After all, we've spent the better part of three months filling our cup (literally and figuratively).

When I was young, some of my summers were spent picking cherries in the local orchards, easily the quickest way to make some extra money during the harvest. Part of another summer was spent in Alaska, harvesting the bounty of salmon that comes forth each July. Yet other summers were spent tirelessly twisting and arranging wedding flowers, weekend after weekend, utilizing the bounty of currants, sunflowers, lamb's ears, and lavender from a friend's garden. Most recently, summers are spent at Le Chalet, working toward the harvest.

Harvests come at all different times, of course. The tomatoes in late summer . . . the peas in late spring . . . the cabbages throughout . . . and the animals in the fall. Cliché as it may sound (which I'm told writers should avoid at all costs), to everything there is a season. Especially on the farm! And the summer season is the season of bounty.

I often find myself unable to take it all in. It's as if the richness of these days is more than I can bear. That's not to say that days go by without difficulty, stress, or fatigue, because that's always part of the equation. But beyond the surface-level emotions, and beyond the mess of a kitchen deep in sticky peach juices, sits a bounty that is more than we can possibly enjoy.

Farmers' market stands are filled to the brim with all the goodness our local areas have to offer. The herbs reach up to my waist and the blossoms on the lavender can reach even higher. Neighbors are happy to swing by for a drink and equally as happy to sit outdoors and chat late into the night. Summer, you see, is full of bounty beyond just our vegetable baskets. Summer brings with it a relaxed home, full of fresh air and flowers, that is eager to welcome others.

Summer brings the party, baby. And I'm showing up with bells on.

AUTUMN'S RICHES

*Listen! The wind is rising, the air is wild with leaves, we have
had our summer evenings, now for October Eves!*
—*HUMBERT WOLFE*

I'm not one for re-watching movies, but there are a few excep-
tions in my book. At the top of the list is *You've Got Mail* starring
Meg Ryan and Tom Hanks, which I've watched dozens of times.
Set in New York City, Meg's character is a small children's book-
store owner who celebrates the seasons with read-alouds and festive
decor and displays. In one particular scene, she emails Tom Hanks's
character regarding the smell of New York in the fall and the possibilities of the autumn season, which she likes to celebrate with a
bouquet of newly sharpened pencils.

I totally get it.

Autumn brings with it the desire to stock our school supplies
as well as our larders. Much to the chagrin of my dear husband, I
often find myself waist deep in dreams and projects before we've
even put the garden properly to bed. Let's organize the homeschool
room! Let's repot new houseplants! Let's install a stair runner! Let's

rearrange the couches! Let's do all the things that we've neglected to do over the last six months while we've been playing outside! Let's sharpen every pencil we own!

You know what I'm talkin' about.

Summer sweeps us away and takes us on a romantic vacation where the days are long, the air is warm, and the drinks are cold. Yet when autumn shows up, we're quickly inspired to plunge back into the kitchen, into the comforts of the home, and into the delicious harvest at hand. The only problem I have with autumn is that the riches often outweigh the energy available to take them all in.

Serendipitously, I'm writing this while it actually is autumn. Currently, there is a fire in the living room that smells of cedar and cherrywood. It crackles, pops, and hisses, breaking the dark silence. Dozens of couch pillows and throw blankets are strewn about the floor—remnants of fort-building and an evening spent cozying up together. My feet are snuggled into wool socks that never manage to match. A hot cup of fresh ginger and turmeric root tea, sweetened with our bees' honey, sits beside me to quench my thirst and warm my chest. Stuart reads tales of hobbits to our children, who are dying to know what happens to Smaug the dragon.

Our family gathers twice daily by the fire in the fall. First when we reluctantly pull ourselves from our warm beds to greet each other, our coffee cups, and the day. My kids never sleep past 6:00 a.m. and so the first fire is built when the morning air is still very brisk and chilly before the sun rises. The second fire is built after suppertime, when the dishes are washed, the books are opened, and we've given up on accomplishing anything further that day. It's permission to let everything be until tomorrow. As the fire roars and engulfs the wood, it burns away the tension of the day. It gives us permission to cuddle with babies, read stories, pour extra hot chocolate, and *just be.*

The change of season brings with it changes to the table. As we pull the last of the garden produce from the beds, harvest the animals for meat, and preserve the earth's riches, we're left with cupboards, root cellars, refrigerators, pantries, and larders bursting at the seams. Beautiful jars of plum chutney line the shelves, and curing pancetta hangs from a rack in the kitchen. Blueberries are tucked away in the freezer for pies, and even eggs have been stashed for the dark days of winter.

Lest you think autumn is a time of sheer bliss, it also brings with it a hefty amount of work. Animal pens need to be filled with straw for cold nights. Flower beds need to be mulched to protect tender bulbs. Hoses are rolled up, water heaters are put into troughs, the beehives are put to bed, garden waste is burned, and farm paraphernalia is gathered up from around the property. Plus there are lots of pencil bouquets to sharpen. Naturally.

The Autumn Garden

It is enough
To smell, to crumble the dark earth,
While the robin sings over again
Sad songs of Autumn mirth.
—EDWARD THOMAS

Autumn is not the death of summer. It is a celebration of bounty. It is about milking the last drop out of the day's warmth and holding each vegetable . . . each flower . . . each ray of sun in the very highest regard. It's about filling our homes, bellies, and hearts with what the garden has given us.

Fall is an absolutely delectable time to be in the kitchen preparing dishes, as the gardener gets to use up the odds and ends left in the garden. After all, there are just a few more eggplants, a few more red tomatoes, and if you're lucky, a few more sweet peppers as well. Baskets line the floor of the kitchen and overflow with dirty potatoes, vibrant carrots, and crispy celery. There are freshly cut herbs tied up with old baker's twine hanging here, there, and everywhere. Apples are stashed in large tubs in the root cellar and

the kitchen. Their sweet-tart juices are unrivaled this time of the year and are impossible to resist. The sweet smell of pears dances through the air, and I'm transported to the orchard behind my grandparents' house. Ahh, childhood.

Adulthood brings with it far more work, which is exactly why I spent the better part of August bent over in the garden, amending the soil, planting a variety of fall goodies. It didn't matter how hot it was to work in that summer sun. This was the year I was going to have a beautiful, lush, fruitful fall harvest from the potager. I traded milk with my gardening-guru Grace for some of her cabbage and broccoli starts. Rows of turnips, beets, and carrots were added to the mix. Even lettuces and greens were planted in good faith that we would be nibbling on them all through the autumn and into the start of the cold, dreary winter ahead. Oh man, did I ever work on that fall garden.

And it was *beautiful*. The carrots germinated nicely, the turnips immediately grew into tender delicacies, and even the spinach obliged me by opening its deep green leaves to the sky. Wahoo!

I'm sure every homesteader is giggling right now, because they know what's to come. Rarely does a victory come without a fall on the farm. A fall that would start, let's say, with prized Champagne d'Argent rabbits escaping from their cage. Guess where they decided to enjoy their newfound freedom: The gigantic pasture full of freshly grown hairy vetch and rye grass? The forty million acres of orchard that surround Le Chalet? The pile of alfalfa hay just a few feet from their cage? Nah, that would make too much sense.

In one night, a handful of rabbits managed to undo what had taken me weeks. Every single plant (every single one!) was nibbled to the ground. Heck, they even dug some of them out by the roots! Their vigilance was astounding, and almost admirable. They certainly had good taste.

There have been plenty of moments when I've thrown quite the tantrum when things didn't exactly go as planned. But that's the funny thing about this life: Rarely do things go as planned. So I simply poured myself a glass of red wine and watched the rabbits dart in and out of the garden. Perhaps they felt a little bit of shame. Probably not.

What the rabbits did allow me to do was put the garden to bed a bit earlier than usual. After everything had been harvested, the entire garden bed was covered with a thick layer of old, decomposed hay that would protect it from the harsh winter ahead. The latch on the garden door was closed, and so it would remain for the season.

In a way, saying good-bye to the garden each autumn is like saying good-bye to a friend. You've spent time planning and cultivating it. You've spent time among its rows, picking out weeds that compete with your seeds for space. You've watered and mulched, protected and fertilized. You've filled your baskets to the brim, and dined on your bounty. It's time to pull it all out, only to begin again next year. How perfectly tragic and equally hopeful.

DECORATING FOR AUTUMN OUTDOORS

Someday, when life doesn't involve getting four children to brush their teeth, wash their faces, and make sure they have clean socks on, I'm sure I'll devote more time to decorating outdoors for the season. But for now, I let nature do most of the work, like simply placing an array of pumpkins around the courtyard. It's a great way to get maximum seasonal enjoyment for minimal input! Here are a few more ways to quickly and easily decorate outdoors:

FAVORITE FALL BLOOMERS

Intentionally planting a variety of flowers that bloom in the fall will ensure bouquets of fresh flowers for as long as possible! Here are a few in our garden:

Russian sage	Coreopsis
Mums	Coneflower
Sedum	Globe thistle
Sunflowers	Yarrow
Fall crocuses	Black-eyed
Roses	Susans

Bundles of corn stalks. Broom corn is worth growing just for this. Tie the large bundles to posts or pillars on your porch for rustic, country charm.

Dried flowers and branches. You've got to prune them off the plants anyway, so you might as well put them to use! Go for the drama on this one—large, thick bundles of branches and masses of dried flowers.

Potted mums. This is an easy way to add seasonal color and life to any area! I like to keep my mums all in one color for maximum impact.

Wood crates. Old wooden apple bins are perfect for filling with pinecones and branches, or even for use as planters. They have a wonderful rustic feel to them and can be used almost anywhere.

Seasonal planters. Ornamental kale has always been a favorite of mine. Planted in urns by the front door, with branches and mosses, it will continue to add color and life well into late autumn.

AUTUMN TASKS IN THE POTAGER

The garden requires payment either this season or in the spring. Tasks that we find too cumbersome now will come back to haunt us three times over in the early warm months if we fail to act. Because of this, you'll find many a gardener bent over in the garden, often until the very first deep frost arrives, which seems to be an invitation to let it all rest. There's something particularly cleansing about putting the fall garden to bed, as I rip out and trim back the forest of vegetables and flowers. These beautiful resources have been used and appreciated through the lush growing season, and now their time is done.

I'm perhaps lazier in the fall garden than many gardeners, but I give it my best shot, often employing a small herd of children to help me. In the spring, I'm desperately protective of my tender rows of seedlings and starts, knowing little feet could crush them quite easily. By the autumn, however, the sturdy plants need to be ripped down and removed from the garden bed. And kids are pretty good at that.

To keep the potager in good shape for the coming seasons, here's a quick list to run though:

Remove old annuals. Whether vegetables or flowers, it's time for those annuals to meet the compost pile!

Prune back perennials. Pruning perennials allows their energy to be concentrated in their root systems, keeping them healthy and strong through the cold winter. It also keeps things tidy for the spring, when new growth will emerge.

Amend the soil. Now's the time to layer on some rich compost love to all those beds that have served you well this past growing season.

Mulch the garden beds. Whether you use leaves, straw, pine straw, or rotten hay, mulching the garden beds with a thick layer of organic matter is the equivalent of tucking your child into bed with a warm blanket. It protects tender roots from harsh weather, retains moisture and nutrients, raises the soil temperature, and will begin to break down to feed the soil in the spring.

Clean up. Surely I can't be the only one with Legos, pots, gardening tools, stray socks, mason jars, and seed packets in my garden bed at the end of the season. Now's the time to sweep through, gather them all up, and put them away lest they spend a winter under the snow (only to bother you again in the spring).

WHAT WE'RE HARVESTING ON THE FARM

There is still plenty coming off the vines and from the ground in the autumn, and as many things don't reach maturity until the fall, this just may be your biggest harvest yet! The day I finally decide to pull up all the potatoes, carrots, beets, turnips, cabbages, tomatoes, celery, and dried beans is always a bountiful day. This is the season when the baskets in the kitchen are filled and the refrigerator's contents begin to spill over. Here are some of the delicious goodies rollin' in off the farm:

Apples, pears, and plums. We opt for organic, heirloom varieties from our organic farmer friends and fill our larders to the brim. Varieties that won't store well are turned into dried fruits, sauces, fruit compotes, or pie filling.

Artichokes. Though not our largest harvest, artichokes give their final performance each autumn in a beautiful artichoke tart. The artichokes that remain on the plants, whether intentionally or forgetfully, will begin to flower this season if not picked.

Cabbages. When my life is in order and the stars align, I can plan ahead enough for a fall harvest of cabbages. This is a very good thing around here because I usually put up over fifteen gallons of sauerkraut for winter storage. That's a lot of cabbage!

Grapes. Our favorite winery is just five minutes up the road, and we've often spent weekends there with friends and family. So inspired by our love of wine, we've planted dozens of wine grapes here on the farm as well. As good things do, they'll take

time to mature and develop, but I'm looking forward to our first grape harvest.

Greens. Right before the garden gives way to the heavy frosts, it surges in the production of all kinds of greens such as kale, collards, mustard, spinach, lettuces, and salad mix. Some of the heartier greens, like kale, often stay in my garden after all the remaining plants have been pulled, even through the first few snows!

Herbs. This is the time of year when all the herbs are cut to the ground and either dried or frozen for the months ahead. Some of the herbs, such as thyme, will return in the spring. Most herbs, however, will be replanted the following year. Any sort of tray that allows air to circulate is an easy way to dry herbs. Simply place the tray inside to dry.

Honey. Beekeepers harvest their honey at different times, but we often do a small harvest each fall. After making sure the bees have a more-than-sufficient supply to eat through the winter (this is, after all, *their* honey), we take the remaining frames of honey inside, where they are capped, spun, filtered, and bottled for use the rest of the year. I can't imagine Le Chalet without bees, nor can I imagine warm cups of tea without honey.

Meat. Though it often detracts from the idyllic image people may hold about farm life, harvesting animals for their meat is a reality. Lambs, piglets, old laying hens, rabbits, fattened ducks and geese, and male calves are all ready for harvest. These tasks alone keep us busier than almost any other time of year. Our animals never leave the farm or know the back of a trailer or the inside of a butcher's shop. We birth, raise, kill, butcher, and prepare our animals right here.

To force-ripen green tomatoes, place them in a paper bag with a banana for a few days. The banana produces ethylene as it ripens, which will encourage the tomatoes to ripen as well.

Nuts. For our climate, hazelnuts, almonds, and walnuts are king. I'm thankful that while our trees are maturing, we can still source local nuts from other farmers, as can you in your area. Fresh, local nuts are worth the slightly higher price, even if that means you'll be eating a bit less of them.

Root vegetables. Long tendrils of carrots and parsnips are pulled from the soil, brushed off, and stacked in baskets. Beets and turnips are tugged from their cozy homes, only to be buried once again in boxes of soil for winter storage. It's all-hands-on-deck when it comes to the potato harvest, as eager fingers wiggle through the earth to find the cold, smooth orbs hiding among the mounds. The root vegetables will take center stage on our table from now until spring!

It's extremely beneficial to "activate" nuts to make them easily digestible and get the most nutrition from them. Simply place raw or dry-roasted nuts in a bowl, cover them with water and a pinch of sea salt, and allow them to sit for 8–12 hours at room temperature, before straining off the water and pouring the nuts onto a baking sheet in a single layer. Dehydrate the nuts in an oven on the lowest setting for 12–24 hours until they are dry and crispy.

Squashes. Year by year, we add a new variety to our garden and learn to cook it well. Though some do better in storage than others, they all offer rich nutrition during the bleak winter months (especially when slathered in butter and spices).

Tomatoes. Much as we'd like it to happen, all of the tomatoes will not ripen before the first hard frost that comes in mid-October. Happily, green tomatoes can be used in a variety of chutneys or salsas. They can also be fried, pickled, or even forced to ripen indoors.

Autumn Recipes

 *Gratitude can transform common days into thanksgivings,
turn routine jobs into joy, and change ordinary opportunities
into blessings.* —WILLIAM ARTHUR WARD

As a cook, I always feel richest in autumn. The kitchen is overflowing with the last surge of life from the garden. The result? A marriage between the last of the summer produce and the first of the winter goods. To cook through masses of apples, tomatoes, peppers, squash, and herbs is pure joy.

Autumn is also a good time to gather small handfuls of herbs and tie them together with twine. (The French call these bundles *bouquet garni*.) I store them in a plastic freezer bag, and whenever I need some herby flavors in my cooking, I simply grab a bundle from the freezer.

HOMEMADE CHICKEN AND DUMPLINGS

This recipe takes time, but it's worth it. If you want to skip the time-consuming bit, just start with a rotisserie chicken and canned chicken stock. It won't be as good, but it'll still be wonderful. Right before you're ready to serve, prepare the dumplings. "But how do I prepare dumplings?" you ask. Don't worry. I will tell you. **Serves 6–8**

For the Chicken and Chicken Stock

1 3- to 5-pound chicken

8 cups filtered water

¼ cup cider vinegar

Pinch of peppercorns

A few stalks of celery, a few carrots, a few onions . . . whatever you have lying around

Combine all the ingredients in a large pot or dutch oven. Bring to a simmer, cover, and allow to gently cook for 8–12 hours.

Remove the chicken from the stock, set it aside, and let it cool. Strain the stock to remove any stray bits of bone, skin, or vegetables.

Melt the butter in a large pot. Add the carrots, celery, onion, and a pinch of salt. Sauté until soft and tender, about 10 minutes.

Add the cognac and flour and whisk to combine, taking care to scrape up any browned bits from the pan and to break up any small clumps of flour.

Add the chicken, chicken stock, thyme, a generous pinch of sea salt, and freshly ground pepper. Bring to a simmer, cover, and allow the ingredients to mingle for 20–30 minutes. Season to taste with salt and pepper.

Whisk the ingredients together in a bowl with a fork until smooth and fluffy.

Drop the dumpling dough by the spoonful into the hot, simmering chicken stew. You should be able to fit about 12–15 dumplings into the pot. Cover the pot and allow the dumplings to cook thoroughly, about 15 more minutes.

Garnish with fresh parsley, because it looks beautiful. And that matters.

For the Chicken Stew

4 tablespoons butter

4 large carrots, peeled and cut into ½-inch slices

4 stalks celery, cut into ½-inch slices

1 yellow onion, minced

¼ cup cognac

6 tablespoons all-purpose einkorn flour

Meat from 1 chicken (from making stock), removed from the bone

Reserved chicken stock (from making stock), about 6 cups

1½ teaspoons fresh thyme

Sea salt and freshly ground black pepper

For the Dumplings

2 cups all-purpose flour (I use einkorn)

¾ cup warm whole milk

3 tablespoons butter, melted

1 teaspoon sea salt

1 tablespoons baking powder

BAKED APPLES

One of my family's favorite treats, and by far one of the easiest, is baked apples. Heck, you could even eat them for breakfast. It's a perfect way to use up apples that are a wee bit past their prime. **Serves 6**

Cut the apples in half and use a spoon to scoop out the core. What you're left with is a perfect little hole to fill with a delicious filling. Which is exactly what we're going to do.

In a food processor, combine the remaining ingredients. Pulse to combine to the texture of your choosing.

Scoop a spoonful of the nut filling into the hole of each apple. If there is extra filling, fear not! You can pile those apples high with topping.

Place on a parchment-lined baking tray and bake the apples in a 350°F oven for 40 minutes or until completely soft.

Serve the baked apples with a drizzle of maple syrup and freshly whipped cream. If you're into that sort of thing (I am!).

3 organic apples

⅓ cup butter

¼ cup dehydrated whole cane sugar, maple syrup, or honey

½ teaspoon vanilla extract

1 teaspoon cinnamon

Pinch of salt

1 cup nuts, such as almonds or hazelnuts (soaked and dehydrated are best)

BAGUETTES

When you get accustomed to the scent, texture, and flavor of *fresh* bread . . . it's hard to enjoy anything but. This baguette recipe makes it easy to enjoy fresh bread daily. It's the overnight rise that brings the magic. **Serves 6**

4 cups bread flour

2 cups whole-grain einkorn flour

½ teaspoon yeast

3 teaspoons salt

3 cups warm water

In a large bowl, mix the bread flour, einkorn flour, yeast, and salt. Whisk to combine.

Mix in the water with a stiff spatula.

Cover the bowl with plastic wrap and a tea towel, before setting it aside for the night. I like to do this bit after I wash the supper dishes and the next bit after I wash the breakfast dishes the following morning.

The following day, flour a large surface area and scrape the dough out onto it. Dust the dough with additional einkorn flour and bring it all together into a large ball. Then, divide it into 5 equal-size balls of dough.

Preheat the oven to 475°F.

On a heavily floured surface, roll each ball into a long cylinder. Try not to squish all the air out of the dough. Using your fingertips can be helpful with this.

Place each baguette onto a parchment-lined baking sheet, giving them some space to expand.

Bake the baguette in the preheated oven for 15–20 minutes, until golden. If you like a crunchier crust, place a cast-iron skillet in your preheating oven. Right before you put the baguettes in, throw a few ice cubes into the skillet to create steam. The key to the perfect baguette is a *hot* oven! The longer you preheat, the better. An hour is optimal.

BREAD WITH CHOCOLATE

The first time I had bread with chocolate was in France in my early twenties, when two friends and I backpacked our way through France, Italy, and Spain. Since that trip a decade ago, I still long for the warm, soft bread that is peppered with chunks of dark chocolate. But now I make it myself. **Serves 4**

2 cups warm whole milk

1½ teaspoons yeast

2 tablespoons dehydrated whole cane sugar

4 tablespoons butter, softened

2 teaspoons sea salt

1½ cups whole-grain einkorn flour (or flour of choice)

3 cups organic all-purpose flour (or flour of choice)

6 ounces bittersweet dark chocolate, chopped into small pieces

2 tablespoons butter, melted

In a stand mixer, combine the milk, yeast, sugar, and softened butter. Allow the mixture to sit for 10 minutes, until frothy.

Add the salt and the flours. Using the dough hook, knead the mixture for 5 minutes, until elastic and smooth. The dough should be pulling cleanly off the sides of the bowl. If it's not, add a bit more flour. Then, add the chocolate and mix again to incorporate it deeply into the dough.

Cover the mixing bowl and allow the dough to rise for 2 hours.

Scrape the dough out of the mixing bowl and use buttered hands to gently divide it into 4 even pieces. Carefully stretch or roll a piece of dough into an oval shape, about 6 inches wide and ¾ inch thick. Move the oval onto a piece of parchment paper and repeat with the remaining 3 pieces of dough.

Gently brush the surface of the loaves with the melted butter. Cover the loaves and allow them to rise for another 1½ hours.

Preheat the oven to 375°F.

Carefully lift the parchment paper and loaf onto a baking sheet (you can usually fit 2 loaves per baking sheet). Bake for 15–18 minutes, until golden and fragrant. Best eaten warm with a strong espresso at hand.

PUMPKIN PUREE

This recipe is for those times when you would enjoy scooping pumpkin more than opening a can. There are good pumpkins for turning into pumpkin puree and *better* pumpkins for turning into pumpkin puree. Generally, the smaller to medium-size pumpkins still have dense flesh, so go for them.

15 ounces of pumpkin puree (from two small pumpkins)

Preheat the oven to 375°F.

Start by cutting off the top and the bottom of the pumpkins. Chop, chop, my friends. From there, quarter each of the pumpkins.

Use a spoon to scoop out all of the seeds and the weird stringy stuff that clings to them. (You can roast the seeds and eat them later!)

Set all of the pumpkin quarters on a baking tray and place them in the oven for 40–50 minutes, until the pumpkin is fork-tender. Remove the pumpkin from the oven and let it cool.

Whip out your spoon again and scoop the flesh away from the skin. Discard the skin and keep that soft, sweet flesh.

Pop the pumpkin into your food processor or high-powered blender (or heck, use your potato masher) and blend until silky smooth. You *can* add a few tablespoons of water, if need be, but err on the side of less water. Water dilutes flavor, baby.

Scoop the smooth, perfect pumpkin puree into a jar and stick it in the fridge until you need it for your pies (or you can freeze it in a plastic bag if you're doing this way in advance).

APPLE BUTTER

One of my favorite ways to preserve apples that have passed their prime, apple butter is easy to make and even easier to enjoy. The smell as the apple butter cooks down is unbearably tempting. **Serves 12**

Wash and core the apples, cut them into quarters, and add them to a large pot. No need to peel.

Add the water, lemon juice, and honey.

Use a small piece of cheesecloth and twine to tie up a bundle that includes the cinnamon sticks, cloves, and allspice berries. This will make it easy to remove the spices later on! Add the bundle of spices and vanilla bean to the pot.

Heat the apples over low heat and cook them until they completely fall apart and turn into mush, about 2 hours, stirring every so often. Allow the apple butter to cook down even further, about 2 more hours, which will help concentrate the flavors. If you like your apple butter even thicker, you can continue to reduce it over low heat until it reaches a consistency you like.

Remove the spice bundle and vanilla bean. If you like a perfectly smooth apple butter, you can use an immersion blender to puree it. If you don't mind a chunkier version, you can leave it as is.

The apple butter can now be water-canned, per your canner instructions, or frozen. That is, of course, assuming you don't want to eat the entire pot straightaway.

5 pounds organic apples

1 cup water

2 teaspoons lemon juice

½ cup honey or dehydrated whole cane sugar

2 cinnamon sticks

10 cloves

5 allspice berries

1 vanilla bean, sliced open, or 2 teaspoons vanilla extract

THE PERFECT BUTTERED MASHED POTATOES

Because this dish is so simple, it relies heavily on the flavors of the ingredients. Use the best organic ones you can find. Local potatoes? Butter from pastured cows? All the better. If you prefer, these potatoes can be made beforehand. That way, there's no last-minute potato-mashing stress when you've got company over. **Serves 6**

5 pounds organic russet potatoes

2 sticks (1 cup) butter, room temperature

4 ounces cream cheese, room temperature

½ cup cream, room temperature

Sea salt and freshly ground black pepper, to taste

Peel the potatoes and cut them into quarters. Slip them into a pot and cover them with water. Add a few generous pinches of salt to the water and bring it to a simmer (*not* a boil, which can waterlog the potatoes). Cover the pot and allow the potatoes to cook until they're extremely tender and fall apart a bit when you poke them.

Pour the potatoes into a colander to drain off the cooking liquid.

Pour the potatoes back into the pot and place them back on the stove over low heat. This will serve to evaporate any residual water left in the potatoes.

Remove the potatoes from the stove and add the butter. Use a handheld potato masher to mash the potatoes together with the butter. The more you mash, the smoother your potatoes will be. Alternatively, you could put your potatoes through a ricer to ensure zero chunks make it through to the end.

Once the butter has incorporated and the potatoes are mashed, add the cream cheese and once again mash the potatoes and cream cheese together until they're completely incorporated.

Add the cream to achieve the perfect, silky texture we're striving for. Mash, mash, mash until the potatoes are perfectly smooth.

Salt and pepper to taste. Remember, these are potatoes! They need salt, and lots of it. Taste-test to make sure they're not falling flat on flavor.

Ta da! Perfectly mashed potatoes that can be served straightaway. If you're not ready to serve them quite yet, spoon the potatoes into a baking dish and set it aside. To reheat the potatoes, dollop them with 4 tablespoons of additional butter and pop them into a 350°F oven for 30–40 minutes, until warm.

WALNUT AND PARMESAN PUFFS

You can try to keep little hands off of these warm puffs, but you won't be able to. It's an unwritten rule that anytime a freshly baked goodie comes out of the oven, children will emerge from near and far to have a taste. **Serves 4-6**

1 cup water

7 tablespoons butter

1¼ cups all-purpose flour (I prefer einkorn)

4 eggs

1 cup shredded parmesan cheese

Small pinch of freshly grated nutmeg

½ cup finely chopped walnuts

Sea salt and freshly ground black pepper, to taste

Preheat the oven the 350°F.

In a medium-size saucepan, heat the water and butter over medium heat. Allow the butter to melt and stir to combine.

Add the flour to the water and butter mixture and stir with a wooden spoon to combine. Continue to stir as the mixture morphs into a small ball of dough. Cook the dough for 1 minute, continuing to stir the entire time, as it begins to smooth out.

Remove the dough from the heat. Add an egg to the dough and stir to combine, until the dough becomes creamy. Repeat with the remaining 3 eggs, adding one at a time and incorporating it completely before adding the next.

Add the cheese, nutmeg, and walnuts. Stir to combine. Season to taste with salt and pepper.

Scoop the dough into a large plastic baggie and cut a small bit off of one of the corners to create a makeshift piping bag.

Squeeze out walnut-size dollops of dough onto a baking sheet lined with parchment paper. They'll puff up when they cook, so give them a bit of elbow room. If you don't want to go to the bother of piping the puffs, just use 2 spoons to scoop the dough out onto the parchment paper much like you would cookie dough.

Bake the puffs for 20–25 minutes, until golden.

ROSEMARY HONEY

Many infused honey recipes call for simmering the honey along with the herbs and then straining the herbs out. We do it a bit differently around here because I like to keep my honey raw, which is when its health benefits are at their highest. I also like to keep the herbs in the honey so that when you spoon the honey onto bread or over meats, you get to enjoy their color and flavor. **Makes 1 cup**

Place the honey and rosemary in a small bowl and stir well to combine.

1 cup raw, local honey

1 tablespoon freshly chopped rosemary

Pour the honey into a glass jar and seal with a lid. Allow the honey to sit undisturbed for at least a week to infuse.

Drizzle the honey over crackers, fruits, roast chicken, fresh bread, roasted vegetables, or whatever tickles your fancy.

Autumn in the Home

 This house is clean enough to be healthy and dirty enough to be happy. —UNKNOWN

I could see it even though my Realtor couldn't. When we first walked through the house on what would become our new farm, it was the kitchen that stood out as particularly awful. Faux oak cabinets, dark green carpet, small windows—this baby had the works! But I saw exactly what it could be. This kitchen had beautiful bones, and I was excited to expose them.

Unfortunately, it was six months before I could finally take a sledgehammer to the whole thing. On a farm, you see, the comfort of our animals comes first, so we spent our first year building their accommodations. It wasn't until summer, when the animals went to pasture, that we were able to dig in (read: take a sledgehammer to the cabinets). Unfortunately, Stuart was the only one who could get rid of all the bits we hated.

What was left was a shell of what had been. Holes littered the walls and ceiling, and the refrigerator and oven sat in the middle of the kitchen. But the room was finally stripped down to its bare self of stucco walls and original tongue-and-groove flooring. I now had a blank canvas to work with.

I wish I could say the next part was like a home renovation show in which everything is magically transformed in a matter of days, but with a farm and four little ones, this wasn't happening. And truthfully, I've discovered authentic cottage style really does take years to layer on. We're not shopping an IKEA showroom here, people (not that there's anything wrong with that). We spent the better part of a year and a half sourcing the perfect pieces, colors, and decor that we wanted to incorporate. Though it's certainly not the easiest way to go, the result is richly satisfying.

One thing I love particularly about this kitchen is that you could hardly mistake it for anyone else's. This space is clearly *Shaye's space*. It's rustic, patched together, crumbly, and imperfect. In other words, perfect.

AUTUMN TEXTILES

One of the easiest ways to transform the summer home into the fall home is to bring out the blankets. Ah, who am I kidding? This isn't a manor. We don't have servants "bringing out" the blankets. What I mean by this is simply putting blankets appropriate for the season on display. Throw blankets, gently strewn over the arm of a couch or chair, are the perfect way to make a room feel comfortable and approachable. It says to the passerby, "Hello there. Care to join me on the couch for a few moments?" at which point the passerby usually has to oblige. Mission accomplished.

What kind of throw blanket person are you? Are you the fold-it-and-lay-it-over-the-top type? Or are you the throw-it-loosely-and-casually-over-the-arm type? I'll confess, I'm a non-folder. I simply drape the blankets over whatever piece of furniture seems right. I like to keep things casual and inviting (also, my kids unfold the blankets every five seconds anyway).

This time of year on the farm, we also layer additional fleece blankets on everyone's beds. A 1909 farmhouse can get a bit drafty, and thus the additional warmth is welcomed. I often think about the unheated homes of the past and how cold the occupants must have been through the fall and winter. I shiver at the thought of it.

Here are a few of my fall favorites:

Plaids. Plaid is practically the dress code for the Pacific Northwest. Plaid textiles are a beautiful and easy way to add autumnal richness to your home. Plaid pillows, plaid throw blankets, plaid tablecloths . . . you get where I'm going with this, right?

When Stuart and I were getting to know each other, I told him I liked a blue plaid scarf he owned. "It's a tartan," he said. "So like a blue plaid then?" I asked. "Kind of. But a tartan." This went on for a while.

Turns out, I had fallen in love with a proud Scottish descendant of the Elliot clan, which has its own tartan. Stuart has a soft spot for this tartan from his ancestors' native country. He'd love nothing more than Elliot tartan throw blankets and wallpaper. Unfortunately for him, the bright blue doesn't match the current color palette. Sorry, honey.

Wool. My kids call it itchy, but I don't care. I still have a deep affection for wool. Perhaps it's because we raise sheep or perhaps it's because the best secondhand blankets are always made of wool. They're warm and long-lasting.

Vintage quilts. Nothing adds instant charm and comfort quite like a quilt. Because I don't make quilts, nor do I know anyone who does, all my quilts have been collected from vintage markets and thrift stores over the years. I always wonder who made them. How many hours did they spend sewing their seams and patterns? How many people have the quilts warmed with their beauty? (Which is also why I always hand-wash secondhand quilts in the bathtub before using. Ha!)

DIY DROP CLOTH CURTAINS

Once upon a time, I wanted to put curtains over my gigantic living room windows. So, as I do, I began to shop around for a style with the perfect amount of farmhouse and the perfect amount of chic. I found some that would've been perfect, but to the tune of two thousand dollars. That's a wee bit too much chic for this farmer. So instead, I grabbed drop cloths from the local home-improvement store and spent two hundred on the entire project. Mission accomplished. Here's how you can, too.

Measure your room from floor to ceiling. You'll want to look for a drop cloth that's 12 inches longer than this measurement so that you have extra to fold over and a small amount to pool on the floor once the curtain is made.

Canvas painter's drop cloth

Double-sided carpet tape

Curtain rod

Wash and dry the drop cloth. This helps to remove creases and loosen up the fabric a bit; it's naturally a bit wrinkly. It's part of its charm.

Lay the drop cloth out on a clean floor with the back of the canvas facing up. Fold the top of the canvas 8 inches back over itself, creating a pocket for the rod to go through.

Lay down a strip of carpet tape right next to and parallel to this line. Pull the rod pocket fabric a bit farther so that it will reach the tape strip. Press firmly across the entire length of the curtain.

Congratulations! You've just created the easiest drop cloth curtain known to man.

Hang the curtain rod according to package instructions before threading the rod through the pocket you created.

Drop cloths look beautiful puddled just slightly on the floor and gathered together by a tieback or curtain rod on the edge of the window. For these windows, I've simply added a wide ribbon that's been tacked in the back.

COTTAGE ELEMENTS FOR AUTUMN

As I've mentioned, I'm not a huge player with seasonal decor. In other words, you won't find a blow-up scarecrow in our front yard (not that there's anything wrong with that). So when autumn rolls around and I'm wanting to welcome it to the farm, I rely pretty heavily on one item in particular: the pumpkin, of course.

Just up the road is a friend and neighbor we call "Farmer Steve." Farmer Steve was one of the first people to help us get set up with pigs and let us gather fruit from his orchards when we didn't have much money to spare. We've helped him with various farm projects, and he's provided us with some pretty delicious produce.

I've yet to pull up to Farmer Steve's and not have a litter of piglets greet me. Oh my word, do I love piglets! In addition to pigs,

Farmer Steve grows and sells *a lot* of pumpkins. Each year, the little ones are bundled up in their flannels and farm boots before we pack them into the car for the two-minute drive to his farm. The vintage "Pumpkin Patch" sign greets us, and before the car has come to a complete stop, the kids are scratching at the windows to get out. There are, after all, pumpkins to claim.

Stuart always takes charge of the pumpkin-carving, and while he and the kids chisel out scary eyes and toothy grins, I get to work placing pumpkins around the courtyard and inside the house. A few always find their way to the stairs leading up to the front door, and a few more are casually clustered around the gates into the courtyard. More will be placed around the potager beds to make up for all the flowers that have faded, and the last few will be placed in the pots that frame the outside of the kitchen door. Inside, smaller pumpkins dot end tables, mantels, and cabinets.

What makes pumpkins so perfect for cottage decor is that they're seasonal, unfussy, almost unbreakable, and imperfect. Are you catching on to the theme of this book?

Easy, Small Touches

There are a few small ways to quickly add a beautiful touch to the autumn farmhouse. After all, when you're busy putting up the last of the harvest, mulching the flower beds, and baking pies, you don't have too much time to spare. When I'm getting ready to freshen a space for a new season, I often ask myself: How do I want to feel when I walk into this room?

If I want to feel comfort, for example, I layer on extra throw blankets and pillows, cluster some candles together, and add live plants, flowers, or silk curtains. All of those elements add a feeling of warmth to a space, which is most welcome in the chilly and dark season of autumn.

Candles. There's nothing like the warmth that comes from candles. The glow is radiant and brings a soft, comfortable hue to the space. My very favorite candles are made from pure beeswax, which purify the air as well as beautify the space. I like to keep candles in clusters in varying heights to add interest and impact. I avoid artificially scented candles because I want my home to smell like a natural farmhouse! And to me that means a pot of soup, a loaf of freshly baked bread, and beeswax candles.

Wreaths are one of my favorite ways to add florals to a room. Their circular shape contrasts with the sharp edges of tables and doorways and adds visual interest to a room. Grapevine wreaths and preserved boxwood wreaths are two of my favorites. They're simple, unfussy, and usable all year round.

Florals. Whether in the form of flowers from the potager, branches from a tree, or even silk flowers, adding a layer of florals quickly transforms a space into a place where life exists. This could be flowers in a vase on the table, potted herbs brought in for the season, or even a container of greens pruned from the tree. No need to make it fussy.

Layers. Autumn is the perfect time to layer extra stacks of books, extra crystals on the chandeliers, and extra pieces of wood by the fireplace. These small details can make a room feel bountiful and beautiful.

Vintage Chandeliers

An old friend of mine spent almost twenty years building her collection of chandeliers that now adorn almost every room in her home. Somehow, she was able to marry them with wooden crates of potatoes and rusted metal signs. Just like sugar and salt complement each other in the kitchen, so it was with her chandeliers and other decor. Even so, I spent years *avoiding* buying chandeliers because I was convinced they were far too fussy for my rustic spaces. So instead, I bought regular light fixtures and hated them all!

I can't quite remember now how I ended up with my first vintage French chandelier. It was small, antiqued, and adorned with tear-shaped crystals. The instant Stuart hung it up, I knew that every hanging light fixture would now have to be replaced.

I've had the best luck finding chandeliers from secondhand retailers online. Most often, they come from somewhere in Europe. This sometimes requires a bit of work to switch out the lightbulb sockets to American sizes, but it can easily be done with a trip to the home-improvement store. I've happily collected five chandeliers so far, and I hope they're passed down to my great-grandchildren.

**WHAT I LOOK FOR
IN A CHANDELIER**

VINTAGE: Victorian style
is my favorite.

METAL: Typically brass.

CRYSTALS: I know they seem
fussy, but trust me
on this one.

We're remodeling the rest of our rooms so that a vintage chandelier can be displayed in each one. Sometimes the influence of a friend can be a very, very good thing.

DECORATING CHANDELIERS

A fun way to mark the change of seasons is to decorate the chandelier that hangs over our dining room table. This year it was all about cream-colored silk roses and dried flowers and leaves from the potager. It makes the room feel so festive! My older daughter almost lost her mind with excitement. I guess creative juices trickle down generationally.

Begin by building a structural base on the chandelier that you can incorporate other elements into, kind of like making a wreath. This is done by winding the silk branches around the arms of the chandelier and wiring them into place. Shorten the stems of the branches by cutting them, if need be, so that they're not poking out anywhere.

Silk branches of choice

Silk flowers of choice

Wire

Variety of dried flowers and leaves

Add your focal flowers. These are the flowers that will catch your eye. They could easily be dried roses, sunflowers, or hydrangeas from your garden. Again, cut the stems of the flowers so they don't poke out, and wire the flowers into place.

Wire anything else you'd like to add. This year, I used a combination of dried yarrow, oak leaves, rose hips, and Spanish moss. You're only limited by your imagination, so use whatever you have on hand to make it festive.

Finish the chandelier off with dangling ornaments or ribbon, if you'd like. Allow those creative juices to flow, and you'll be amazed at what can come out!

ELEMENTS OF MY COTTAGE KITCHEN

Copper. Oh copper, how I love thee! I've been building my copper collection for a decade now, and in copper world, that's a very short time. Most of these pieces are collected from French online retailers who source vintage copper, refinish it, and resell it. I've since made friends with a coppersmith who lovingly re-tins and polishes my pots and pans as the tin lining wears through. This is a lost art I am happy to support. I opt for the pots and pans that are at least 2 millimeters thick, for optimal structural and temperature support. I still have a few pan sizes to save up for, but in the meantime, there's still plenty to enjoy. Our thrift-store copper rack keeps it all gathered together nicely over the stove for maximum visual impact. There is simply nothing that compares to the rich, warm glow of copper.

The kitchen couch. Is it just me, or does *everyone* seem to hang out in the kitchen with Mom? My posse is so ever-present that I decided the heck with it and I put a couch in the kitchen. Now people have a place to sit versus lingering around the stove, driving me bonkers. When I added the couch, I didn't expect the richness it would add to our everyday fellowship. Turns out, I spend *a lot* of time in the kitchen, and this way, whoever needs me or wants to talk has a quick and comfortable place to rest while they do so. Company can enjoy a glass of wine while I finish up supper, kids can have a place to nap if need be, Stuart and I can squeeze a few moments in together with our morning coffee, and, of course, Mama has a place to collapse after supper dishes if she can't drag her old, weak bones all the way to the living room. I'm sure we'll have to replace the couch from wear and tear, but I can hardly imagine my kitchen without it now.

The stove. I remember the first time I saw the French range we now own. I wanted to weep. It was so *beautiful*. I spent about

a year saving for this range, and another five months waiting for it to arrive from France. Hardly instant gratification . . . but my-oh-my was it worth the wait! And while it may seem like a buzzkill to spend so much of the renovation budget on this one piece, I knew that I was looking at decades of cooking every day with it. I ran the math, and as it turns out, it only costs me cents per day to cook on this range for the duration of its life. And let's be honest, I'll probably go before it does.

The industrial refrigerator. We were lucky to snag our gigantic industrial refrigerator from a local espresso stand that was going out of business. Here's the thing: When you're harvesting lots of meat, milking a cow, growing your veggies and fruits, and feeding four children, you need *a lot* of fridge space. This beast allows us to store the bounty from the garden and still have room for leftovers. We keep three freezers in our basement for frozen goods.

Meat racks. Before refrigeration, most meat was cured. Salt was used to remove some or all of the water from the meat, at which point it could be hung or stored for future use. We harvest pigs each autumn, and our meat racks are once again filled with salt-cured goodies like prosciutto, guanciale, salami, chorizo, bacon, Canadian bacon, pancetta, coppa, spalla, and more. We store the majority of the meat in the root cellar, where it is drier and cooler, but always keep one of each on hand in the kitchen for quick access.

Stacks of plates. It's important to us that Le Chalet be a place where others are always welcome to join us at mealtime. With all the relatives, neighbors, and church family we have nearby, there are almost always extra mouths to feed—sometimes planned, sometimes not. So that's also why I keep a stack of thirty plates. You never know.

Note: Our kitchen is lacking a few "standard" essentials like a toaster, microwave, and dishwasher. We've found none of these to be necessities and opted instead for the additional space their absence brings.

There's no *one* thing that makes a cottage kitchen. Rather, it's a little of this or that, each building upon another. A kitchen can be a beautiful reflection of its owner, exposing tastes, styles, and aspirations. Here on the farm, we know a few things: It's got to be rustic, it's got to be useful, and it's got to be beautiful.

Hand-Washing Dishes

I can already hear the moans coming from the crowd on this one, but hear me out. Our kitchen originally came equipped with an older dishwasher that was used every so often. In comes our herd and within a few weeks, the dishwasher was running two cycles a day. As these things go, it eventually gave out, but instead of replacing it with another model, we did something *radical*. We decided to wash by hand. Now, remember if you will, we have four children. That's a lot of dishes!

As a young girl, I remember watching my mom, aunts, and grandma wash dishes. After a family meal or holiday celebration, the women would assemble back in the kitchen. Someone would scrape and rinse, someone would wash, someone would dry, and someone would stand at the counter, sipping wine and trying to look busy. My mom and all her sisters were meticulous washers. I remember many conversations about this task: Which way should the silverware go into the soapy water, handle toward or away from the person washing? Which items should be submerged and which should be washed with a soapy rag? Thrilling conversations, I tell you. But at the end of it all, the dishes came out sparkling. "The difference between a good washer and a bad washer is the dryer," my grandma would say.

I get why people don't want to spend more time in the kitchen. But I also understand the benefit that comes from such a task. It forces us to slow down and to work together to accomplish a goal. It allows the little ones to get involved and learn a new skill. *Plus*, no one has to unload the dishwasher, which we all know is the worst chore in the history of the world.

Caring for Copper

You may have noticed I have a deep love affair with copper. It dangles from the ceiling, sits on the shelves, and is utilized all day, every day. Stuart bought me my first copper pan from a vintage store back in the day, and it's been all roses and sunshine ever since. In another life, I would've been a coppersmith and spent my days re-tinning and polishing vintage finds, all the while firing new ones for future generations. How many things nowadays can be passed down from generation to generation? I'm banking that my copper and cast iron will be the only things that survive the hurricane of my little ones.

After many online searches, I was fortunate to find an American women living with her coppersmith husband in France. Each month, she hosts online pop-up sales through which lucky consumers can purchase one of his restored pieces. Month by month, I've been building my copper collection. Isn't it a cool world?

Copper takes on a natural patina as it reacts to various things in the environment, and I am crazy about the looks it takes on. That being said, a few times a year, I like to show my copper a bit of extra love by polishing it. My kids jump in on the party and the process goes quickly. There are lots of ways to polish copper. Here are my favorites:

- Brush the copper down completely with tomato sauce. Let it sit for 30 minutes and then wash it off.

- Mix 1 tablespoon of salt with 1 tablespoon of flour and add enough vinegar to form a paste. Spread this over the copper and allow it to sit for 30 minutes before washing it off.

- Rub the copper down with halves of a lemon dipped in salt. Let sit for 30 minutes and then rinse.

WHAT TO DO WITH SHORTER DAYS

Autumn is the time of year when we spend just a little more time inside. The dark mornings keep us housebound a little later than usual, as does the early sunset. We fill the extra time with noble tasks like folding laundry, scrubbing and painting dirty walls, and washing dishes. When we're feeling slightly more refined, we also fill the long nights with:

Longer meals. Simply because we can, we often linger around the table longer than usual this time of year. An extra glass of wine (or milk) is poured, and we spend more time eating, conversing, and watching the little ones run around the table. We're able to submit slightly to the madness and sip our Bordeaux while they pretend to be lions . . . or sharks . . . or ninjas . . . or whatever it is they are that day. There's no rush to clean up, am I right?

Teatime. My kids eagerly anticipate teatime, most likely because I swirl a hefty spoonful of our honey into the teapot. They're just as excited to enjoy a cup on these chilly days as I am. We pour the tea, stick up our pinkies, and pretend that we're people who are refined enough to do such things. That usually gives us a good laugh.

Good literature. My husband could without a doubt write an entire book on the importance of good literature in a child's life. One of his sole missions in life is to provide our kids with stories that help them understand the world and their place in it. Almost every night the family gathers around to listen to him read, whether it's *The Hobbit*, *A Kingdom Far and Clear*, *The Green Ember*, *Little House on the Prairie*, or Dr. Seuss.

Drawing. My drawing skills are laughable, but when I'm on art-duty, I try to channel my inner Beatrix Potter. Stuart has a much more developed skill and is eager to share that with the kids, so he teaches them things like perspective, shading, and pencil techniques. What a guy.

Singing. Does this make us a weird family? Yes? Oh well, I guess it's a label we must accept. We learn songs as a family and then practice them all week. It fills the space with a joyful noise and provides us a source of entertainment. It's quite fun, though we're still working on the harmonies . . .

Time by the fire. I'm of the mindset that people don't need an excuse to wrap up in a wool blanket, grab a cup of espresso, and do nothing other than watch the fire burn. Try it. Put a fire on. It's absolutely captivating. If you've been blessed with a fireplace, make it the center of your entertainment this time of year! If you haven't, buy a small fire pit to put in the backyard, bundle up, and head outside. Your soul needs time by the fire.

Tech check. A while back, Stuart and I decided that we didn't want our devices to create a barrier between family members or farm life. We don't want our children to see us glued to screens, so we keep such work to a minimum. Likewise, our kids don't do tablets. Or iPods. Or phones. When they're bored, I kick them outside and tell them to go find an adventure. But like other families, we still need to "tech-check" each other every so often. Phones are the biggest culprit, but all it takes is for a family member to say, "Hey. I love you and want to spend quality time with you. Is what you're doing on your phone good and necessary right now?" That'll keep you humble.

GLITTERY LEAF GARLAND

If you're a parent, you probably see the word "glitter" and shudder, but I can't help myself. As rustic a life as I may lead, I love glitter. Tastefully done, of course. It just so happens we have a few magnificent trees on our farm that drop their leaves each fall, creating for us the perfect natural palette on which to sprinkle the sparkles. How can you resist?

Leaves

Rubber cement

Glitter

Natural twine

Wipe the leaves clean with a rag, so that they're dry and no debris remains.

Brush a very thin layer of rubber cement over one leaf. Sprinkle the leaf with glitter of your choosing. Because of the beautiful shades of autumn at play in the cherry trees around our farm, I most often opt for gold. How fancy.

Shake the excess glitter from each leaf and allow it to dry.

Cut a piece of twine the length that you'd like your garland to be. Then, cut a bunch of other pieces of twine 2 inches long.

Tie each leaf by its stem onto the long piece of twine, using the shorter pieces of twine, to create a garland, which can be placed anywhere your farmhouse needs a bit more pizzazz.

Congratulations! You're now your children's favorite parent in the whole world.

THE COLORS OF AUTUMN

Without question, autumn colors are my favorite. They're rich and warm, like red wine and copper. The orchards surrounding Le Chalet light up in a fury as the nights get longer and the days cooler. The cherry trees transform into the most decadent shade of yellow, before transforming into a deep orange. It's a magnificent display that lasts no longer than a week, but absolutely tickles my fancy. When the fall colors come out to play, my heart pumps just a wee bit faster in anticipation of such beauty.

I love these shades so much, in fact, that they are the predominant colors in our home year-round. There's the deep burgundy couch, a reupholstered piece from the 1920s, and another in gold. The area rugs are full of browns, reds, and taupes. Copper planters litter the tables, bringing a particular warmth to the space. The wood trim that edges the doors and windows is made from local fir, which turns a rosy shade of orange as it ages.

I think the very best part of these fiery shades is the warmth they impart. Unlike whites, grays, and silvers, autumnal shades say, "Come in and let me warm your bones." Yes, please!

Autumn Celebrations

 With good friends . . . and good food on the board . . . we may well ask, When shall we live if not now? —M. F. K. FISHER

This time of year, indoor meals lend themselves to intimate discussions over creamy pastas, slow-roasted meats, and candlelight. Everyone seems prepared to gather in the fall. Perhaps it's the cooler days and nights that draw us in, or perhaps it's the back-to-school routine that drives our schedule. However you slice it, autumn was *made* for gathering and feasting.

As a young girl, I looked forward to the fall holidays that were the basis for many family get-togethers. Cousins, grandparents, aunts, and uncles all made it a point to spend, at the very least, Thanksgiving together. I knew that there would be delicious snacks before the meal (for keeping us little ones happy) and perfectly whipped and buttered mashed potatoes (my favorite food as a child), and that my grandpa would make the gravy the majority of the food would be bathed in. No complaints here.

These meals were a way of shaping my character as a child. The smells, the tastes, and the sounds all worked to create an emotional

imprint of belonging. Who can eat turkey and stuffing without it conjuring up all sorts of memories? Autumn is a particularly special time for gathering in a way that feeds our nostalgia and our bellies. So let's do just that.

THE TABLE

I've said it before and I'll say it again: I'm not much for fussy tables. This is real life where real people eat meals together. And while the magazines and online photographs are certainly beautiful, the reality is there are usually a dozen children wrapped around our table. How could I ever want it any other way? I couldn't. But while I may not adhere to Martha Stewart's standards of table setting, I certainly do believe in setting the stage for the enjoyment of a meal. Here are a few things that always make our table more comfortable:

> **Open bottles.** We want our table to say to people, "Sit, enjoy, and fill your cup again and again." Open bottles of wine, water, or other beverages keep it casual and inviting.

Candlelight. If you have little ones at the table, make sure your candleholders are sturdy! I have only a few that make their appearance over and over again because of this. Candlelight creates magic. Opt for unscented candles whose aroma won't interfere with that of the meal.

Linens. They don't have to be ironed or matching, just make sure they're clean! I still always opt for table linens, even though they're totally impractical with children, because they make a table feel homey and approachable. Stains? Small holes? No bother. I often purchase my linens at thrift stores knowing very well my family will make sure they're damaged and stained in no time.

Oftentimes, it's the smallest things that can create the biggest impact, even if it's far from fancy. Let's break down this photograph, as an example:

The entire table of goodies for entertaining required no cooking on my part. It's an assortment of cheeses, nuts, fruits, olives, and cured meats that are simply presented for guests to enjoy. The "tablecloth" is made from repurposed brown craft paper that came in a shipping package a few days prior. The serving plates were ones I already had on hand. I displayed the cheeses and meats on a variety of platters to keep it interesting. A bit of freshness, such as the grapes and sage garnishes, makes the table feel vibrant and alive.

One of my favorite sayings comes from a designer who constantly encourages her clients to "use what you've got!" I often feel pulled to the store to find the perfect this or that before getting on with decorating for a holiday. Luckily, that saying has stuck with me, and instead of shopping, I grab some branches, leaves, fallen acorns, small pumpkins from the garden, old linens from the drawers, and potted plants from around the house to create a beautiful space for our family to enjoy their meal. It's not about buying more stuff or creating a magazine-worthy spread (those are totally fake anyway). It's about taking what you have, celebrating the simple beauty in it, and learning to make it work for you (even if that means borrowing all of your mom's matching glasses and plates for the day).

THE HOPE OF NEXT YEAR

I will confess that our tomato patch is larger than it needs to be, and, frankly, this is often a point of contention between Stuart and me. We're always in ridiculous battles about what sort of trellising system we'll use and how we'll make it a better and more efficient operation. Yet without fail, the tomatoes grow larger than we initially planned and swallow up half the garden in the process, while we're still bantering back and forth. My first few ripe tomatoes seem to go to the slugs, as they hide out under the feet of the fresh green foliage. By the end of the season, the tomato patch looks like it's been trampled by a flock of geese after I've maneuvered clumsily among the crowded walkways and crushed tender branches in the process.

"Don't worry, love. We'll get 'em next year." These simple words have become our mantra as gardeners, homesteaders, and home cooks. Sure, the mole ate the roots of the celery, the rabbits nibbled the skin off of all the beets and potatoes, and the children somehow managed to eat every single raspberry before any made it into the kitchen. The pitcher of water spilt all over the Thanksgiving table, and I burned the beef Wellington slightly.

But don't worry. We'll get 'em next year.

In creating the farm life, it is always comforting to think of another year filled with possibilities and beauty. When a crop fails, there is the hope that through the experience and loss, a deeper wisdom will be gained and used to implement changes the next season. Problem is, of course, there is no end to the troubles that can befall us as we work the soil, harvest its riches, prepare bountiful dishes, and create a beautiful home in which to enjoy them. The kids will accidentally tear your favorite wool blanket as they build a fort in your beautifully curated living room. Vintage baskets will begin to come apart, your opinion on paint colors will change, and the chandelier bulbs will surely burn out. But that doesn't really matter. Because we can make a honey latte, step outside to soak up the last of the sun's warm rays, and know that there's a beautiful season ahead to care for such matters.

Despite the barren end of autumn, there is still much life to be had through the coming winter.

WINTER'S WARMTH

Laura felt a warmth inside her. It was very small, but it was strong. It was steady, like a tiny light in the dark, and it burned very low but no winds could make it flicker because it would not give up. —FROM THE LONG WINTER BY LAURA INGALLS WILDER

I've spent many winters in the Pacific Northwest, yet the cold never ceases to surprise me. I shiver in the air's chill. *Woo! Baby, it's cold out there!* You'd think I'd be acclimated to it by now, but deep cold still takes my breath away. The laws of science confirm that ice will begin to collect on the single windowpanes, animal troughs will freeze over, flowers will remain in a state of dormancy so deep it tastes of death, and the driveway will require almost daily plowing to prevent the buildup of snow and ice. It is, after all, winter.

Bleak and cold as it may be outside, the beautiful contrast of the season is the warmth and comfort found indoors. Unlike the summer home, airy and open to the world, the winter cottage turns inward. For the introvert, there's hardly a better time of year. People venture out less often (they're not willing to put on long johns, coveralls, scarves, mittens, and wool hats) and are comfortable using the

down time to recharge for the coming year. Recharging, of course, means different things to different people. While Stuart's keen to spend the long, dark hours catching up on reading or art projects, I'm much more inclined to tear into the house plans that I've been neglecting. Don't worry: We're both good at compromise.

Though winter can seem terribly long and boring, it's one of the most dynamic seasons of all. The very first days of winter are filled with excitement as we rush around making holiday plans that include elaborate parties. All manner of greenery, sparkles, and decorations are brought into the home to "deck the halls." This is a huge kickoff as we feast and focus on merriment to our heart's content. Pour the champagne! Glaze the ham! Bring out the chocolates! It isn't until after the rush and bustle of the holidays pass that we begin to settle into the calm, quiet, and peaceful winter rest that will remain until the very first breath of spring.

The Winter Garden

I wonder if the snow loves *the trees and fields, that it kisses them so gently? And then it covers them up snug, you know, with a white quilt; and perhaps it says, "Go to sleep, darlings, till the summer comes again." —LEWIS CARROLL*

Is there a winter garden? In some parts of the country, most certainly. Winter gardens push forth cold-hardy greens and root crops that can stand the frigid nights and short days. That is, of course, unless you live where I do. Winter gardens around here consist of little more than some hardy herbs and the last of the small kale leaves plucked from the stalks. Baskets of produce, all shades of the rainbow, are a distant memory of a season when we didn't have to wear two pairs of socks with our boots to keep the frostbite at bay. Our garden is most definitely *asleep*.

And yet, while the garden slumbers, the gardener dreams. When the ground is frozen and unaccepting of new life, I find joy in recounting successes from the past season and planning new ones for the season ahead. This is almost better than the real deal because as I plan, design, and dream, all the vegetables and flowers

come to life in my head. Regardless of the garden's failings last year, this is the season I can pretend that all of my elaborate fantasies can become reality.

As the snow falls, our harvest no longer comes from the soil but from the root cellar and pantries. Lined with mason jars of canned fruit, fermented vegetables, cured meats, and dried herbs, our root cellar provides us with the majority of our food needs until the spring, supplemented by the occasional trip to the grocery store. It's a daily celebration of the hard work that went into producing the food. While the season of no gardening can be painful for the gardener, it's a time that she can appreciate what the garden has already given. Instead of filling our produce baskets, we fill our bellies on past harvests.

Stocked only with foods I love, my root cellar is my "farm grocery store." A large room with stone walls and a dirt floor, the cellar, built in 1909, sits directly below the kitchen. Stairs lead from the kitchen right down into the dark room, which is only lit by a small bulb. In the cellar we keep large shelves full of preserves and produce. Prior to this house, I desperately longed for a root cellar that would display crates of wine, links of salamis, braids of onions, baskets of apples, and jars of jelly, with funky, colorful pumpkins, squashes, and dried flowers lining the staircase. I could amble down with a basket each day to grab a bit of our daily provisions. How dreamy!

It took a bit of work to get our root cellar where I wanted it to be. Multiple walls were removed, the staircase was widened, the floor was regraded and graveled, a walk-in cooler was built into one of the two rooms, and a slew of storage shelves were constructed. Now, our root cellar is home to everything we put up from the farm each year and more.

SEED SHOPPING

I often do my seed shopping on the winter solstice, the shortest and darkest day of the entire year. It's a bit of a victory, as if to say, the darkness has not won! From here on out, the days will get longer and the nights shorter as we inch toward the summer solstice, when long stretches of sunshine will again grace the garden.

Everyone has their favorite method of seed shopping, no doubt, but here is mine: I take all of my seed catalogues, draw a nice bath, and spend time looking through each one. With a large red pen in hand, I circle the varieties that make the cut. After that, I place a few online orders. I try to do this early in the winter, so that the varieties I want aren't sold out and so I can have them in hand as early as possible. There's hardly a more exciting day in the barren winter than when the packages of seeds arrive. They're full of hope! Full of possibilities!

PLANNING THE POTAGER

Winter is the perfect time to plan out new garden beds for the coming year. It seems that each year, we add more and more cottage-style beds, and each year I'm left dreaming in January of what is to come. There are as many ways to plan a potager garden as there are stars in the sky, but don't let that overwhelm you. Much like Monet, I often draw my garden plans with just blobs of color or height, rather than specific varieties or plantings (sorry, Monet, for comparing your priceless art to my garden doodles). I find that my mind works best off of height and color, so that's how I plan. Here are a few basic "rules of thumb" that can help you design a beautiful potager:

> **Choose a focal point.** First, potagers do best with a focal point. It could be a birdbath, a bench and a tree, a statue, a barrel of flowers, anything. In our potager, we have a standalone

dogwood tree that gives the eyes a place to rest. A focal point also serves to add structure and interest during the barren winter.

Vary heights. In each of your beds, make a list or drawing of what will grow close to the ground, low to the ground, high up from the ground, and towering over the ground! There should be a good variety of height in every bed, which will create layers of beauty.

Consider bloom time. It's nice to have color in the potager as long as possible, so alternating bloom times within a bed is ideal. Tulips, for example, bloom in the spring. Plant them alongside something that will bloom in the summer, such as hydrangea, to keep the color coming! A garden, in my humble opinion, can never have enough color.

Add charm. Potager gardens need charm. Skip the prefab pavers and opt instead for locally gathered (most likely imperfect) rocks. Skip new patio furniture and opt instead for rusty wrought iron. Work in wind chimes, aged barrels, rustic buckets, or old benches. Use an old wooden ladder as your pea trellis or old chairs as your bean supports. As you spend the dark, cold days of winter thinking about the work and life to come in the spring, think about how you can transpose beauty—the accents, colors, and textures you're madly in love with—into your beds. *That's* the charm you're looking for.

Sketch it out. All that's left now is to sketch it out (and I use "sketch" in the vaguest sense of the word). A few pieces of paper and a colored pen or two is all it takes to get thoughts into physical form. I'm a pitiful drawer, but I can manage enough to get my thoughts onto paper. This helps me see how colors, heights, and bloom times come into play and also helps me develop the shape and flow of the garden beds together. We're in the process

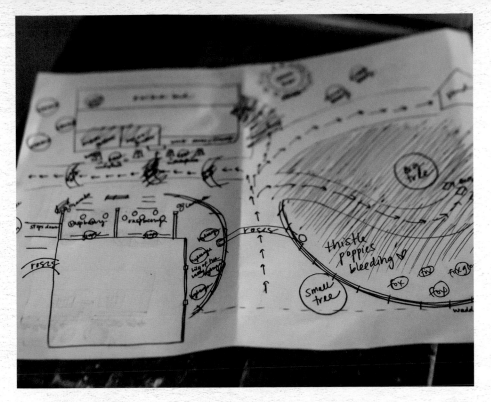

of developing over a thousand square feet of new potager beds surrounding our (new to us) greenhouse, and I currently have half a dozen sketches for how to fill and work the space best. This is your time to dream. Run with it!

GARDEN SUPPLIES

Winter is the perfect time to take inventory of what garden supplies you have and what you'll need for the upcoming year. It wasn't until a few years ago that I finally invested in some gardening tools. Until that point, I'd used anything I could find to get the job done. Funny thing about garden tools is that they're designed for ease of use and a specific job. Sure, you can use a pickax for weeding, but you'll have tired arms at the end of it all. And trust me, I did! So I put on my big-girl pants and splurged on a few tools that will serve me well for years to come. Here's what I find the most useful, and what I make sure I have for the planting season each spring:

- 3¾-inch narrow collinear hoe, for lightweight weeding between planted rows

- 7-inch collinear hoe, for weeding between beds

- Broadfork, for prepping beds

- Trowel, for transplanting seedlings

- Wire weeder, for hand weeding

- Hand hoe, for digging and weeding

- Seeder, for easy and accurate planting

- Biodegradable planting pots

- Pot-labeling sticks

BLOOMING WINTER FLOWERS

Lest you think the winter is without hope, rest easy. There are a few flowers that make their appearance in the super-late fall or super-early spring that will keep you encouraged. Incorporate them into your garden plans for the longest stretch of blooms you can get.

Winter rose 'Hellebore'	Winter jasmine	Ornamental kale
Witch hazel	Daphne shrub	Cyclamen
	Winter aconite	Snowdrops
	Winter pansies	

FEED THE BIRDS

When the winter garden is dusted with snow and the branches of the trees and shrubs are exposed, birdsong echoes off the bare landscape and is all the more beautiful. A slew of birds call our farm home, and we are pleased to have them. These sweet bird feeders are perfect to make with the little ones and can be hung outside your windows so you can watch and observe the birds in all their beautiful winter glory.

Tie a loop of string to the top of each pinecone. This will allow you to hang the cones with ease.

Smear the pinecones entirely with peanut butter. Prepare to get your hands messy!

Roll the gooey pinecones in the bird seed to coat them in the seed mixture. Sprinkle if you must to get all the nooks and crannies.

Hang the pinecones outdoors and watch for the avian magic to come.

String

6 pinecones

2 cups peanut butter

4 cups bird seed, or any combination of sunflower, flax, millet, quinoa, or finely chopped pumpkin seeds

THE FINAL FARM CLEANUP

Try as we might, there's no possible way to keep a farm (or a family, for that matter) totally clean. Garden tools are used as swords and left in the pasture, coffee mugs continually find their way outside, and hats and mittens are strewn about like fallen leaves. We watch weather reports for the first snow of the season, which we look forward to because we know what it means: the final farm cleanup.

All we have to do is ask ourselves one question: Do we want to be digging this out of the frozen snow in the spring? If not, then it's time to pick it up. Tools, stacks of wood, the last of the garden

waste, and children's toys are gathered, sorted, and put away. The brush is often burned in a large bonfire that seems to signal to the snow it's now welcome to arrive.

We often have a few rogue chickens wandering around the farm, chickens who have decided that the gigantic run is simply not enough room for their free spirits. I can always tell when one has escaped because the beds in my potager will be scratched up and soil and plant debris scattered all over the pea gravel. In the late autumn, I let the rogue chickens get their fill of the last of the grubs and creepy crawlies. When the snow is coming, I'll do one final raking of the beds, gather my tools, and put them in the greenhouse, where they'll remain until spring.

It's always bittersweet to do the final farm cleanup. Though winter will bring its own charm, saying good-bye to the last tastes of summer and fall is always a bit sad. I will begin to immediately long for the days when the kids can ride their tricycles down the driveway and build their forts under the trees.

Don't worry. They'll come.

WHAT WE'RE EATING
ON THE FARM

Unlike spring, summer, and autumn, during which we enjoy our
meals alongside our garden tasks, winter is all but silent in the
garden. There are no ripe tomatoes to pluck from the vines and
no fresh peas to pop into the soup pot. What has been grown
and stored on the farm is what's on the menu for the foreseeable
future.

In many ways, winter is a gift, a rest for the weary gardener
who has spent the past nine months toiling in the soil. It is now
time to feast on the fruits of our labor. Winter dishes are often
filled with rustic, gnarled root vegetables and rich meats and
stocks. They lend themselves well to sitting by the fire and large
pieces of buttered, crusty breads. It's a delicious opportunity to
fall further in love with a new, and slightly less appreciated, cast of
characters.

Beets, turnips, and parsnips. Also perfect to keep buried in
potting soil, beets, turnips, and parsnips are a welcome addition
to the winter table. I grow varieties that will keep for the longest length of time.

Cabbages. The majority of my cabbage harvest is put up into
sauerkraut and kimchi, but I do keep some cabbage heads
around for fresh eating. My family's favorite way is an entire
head of cabbage cooked down with *a lot* of butter and salt. Once
the cabbage is soft, we serve it topped with a few poached eggs
and some crumbled bacon. Even storage varieties of cabbage
won't store as long as beets and carrots, but kept covered and
cool, they can at least last until the beginning of winter.

Canned fruit. I can my fruit with honey from our beehives. The result is fragrant, silky fruit that is a decadent treat come February. Pears, peaches, and cherries always make the list, as they lend themselves perfectly to such preservation.

Carrots. Notoriously long-keepers, carrots can last all the way until spring. I bury mine in potting soil, in large plastic crates, and store them in the walk-in cooler, where they will stay the coolest. Then I just dig them out of the soil as I need them.

Cured meats. A huge area of our root cellar is devoted to the cured meats that we put up each autumn from our pigs. It is a dark, cool area, and a small fan keeps the air moving freely. Bacon, prosciutto, pancetta, coppa, spalla, salami, chorizo, and lardo all hang from the floor rafters of the kitchen above. There's hardly anything that'll make a farmer feel richer.

Dried herbs and flowers. Harvested each spring and summer, herbs and flowers will be utilized all winter to flavor our dishes and teas. What is it about this act that feels so magical?

Frozen fruits and vegetables. Whatever vegetables aren't fermented are frozen. Peas, green beans, corn, and broccoli are at the top of my list. To add to that, I freeze a ridiculous amount of blueberries, blackberries, and raspberries each summer. In the cold of the winter, I sprinkle berries over my steaming oatmeal to remind me that the sun will surely shine again. Peaches and apricots are also a welcome addition to winter smoothies or crumbles.

Jams and jellies. Lining the shelves of the root cellar are some of my personal favorites: raspberry-currant jam, apricot jam, rhubarb jam, spiced plum jam, apple butter, pear butter, pepper jelly, and on it goes. It feels like such a luxury to fill my basket with sweet treats that speak perfectly of a season.

Pesto and chutneys. I grow a hedgerow of basil each year purely for the purpose of making a winter supply of pesto, which we mix with pasta or spread over homemade pizza dough. It tastes richly of summer. The chutneys that we store are usually composed of whatever was growing well the season before—usually rhubarb. The chopped rhubarb is slowly simmered with honey, vinegar, onion, dried fruit, and spices and is served over roasted pork or chicken throughout the winter.

Sauerkraut, pickles, and other fermented vegetables. My preferred method of preserving most vegetables is through fermentation. Rather than pickling the vegetables, which all but ruins their nutritional value, fermentation provides additional digestive bacteria. It is said that sailors on ships centuries ago could easily prevent scurvy through the consumption of fermented vegetables, and thus would fill their ships with barrels and barrels of them. I do the same in my root cellar.

Soup bones. After harvesting our animals each fall, we keep the bones in the freezer to be utilized for rich stocks all year long. The bones are added to a large stockpot, which is filled with water, a cup of vinegar, a few carrots, celery, onion, peppercorns, and bay leaves. The stock is then simmered for twenty-four hours and strained. I make stock twice weekly during the cold months, when soup is a necessity.

Squashes. Butternut is an obvious favorite around here. It can be roasted in the oven, drizzled with honey and oil, and dusted with warming spices for delicious side dishes. Certain varieties of squash will keep well into the springtime. I tend to grow varieties for their storage qualities and the sweetness of their flesh. They can be stored in bins around the kitchen and root cellar.

Winter Recipes

The art of bread making can become a consuming hobby, and no matter how often and how many kinds of bread one has made, there always seems to be something new to learn. —JULIA CHILD

I welcome winter into the kitchen with comforting dishes that will warm and nourish us. In fact, there are few places I'd rather be on these chilly days, which is good, because during the winter it's hard to be anywhere else. Bread-making keeps me bound to the kitchen for at least a few good hours, as I knead and mold it to shape. Extra time is spent peeling potatoes and carrots, chopping up the thick-skinned butternut squash, and browning meats.

Unlike the summer, when supper can easily consist of a handful of raw vegetables from the garden, winter food requires roasting, simmering, and searing. This results in deeply flavored dishes with layers of complexity. During this time, I tend to spend my days stirring pots and watching oven temperatures. Frothy, rich hot chocolate is kept nearby at all times to ensure optimal performance and pleasure.

HOT CHOCOLATE

One of the most requested treats in the winter . . . and I certainly don't mind. You'll find me stirring this sweet liquid over the stove almost every morning. **Serves 6**

8 cups whole, organic milk

¾ cup cocoa powder

½ cup maple syrup

Pinch of sea salt

3.5 ounces dark, bittersweet chocolate (optional for a richer hot chocolate)

In a large saucepan, combine the milk, cocoa powder, maple syrup, salt, and optional chocolate.

Heat the mixture until it's not quite boiling, but steaming and melted together, whisking all the while to help dissolve the cocoa and chocolate.

Ladle into mugs and enjoy.

HOMEMADE MARSHMALLOWS

Homemade marshmallows won't save the world or make your children be patient while they wait anxiously for Christmas, but they *will* make your homemade hot chocolate or honey latte that much better. And that counts for something, right? **Makes about 2 dozen**

In a small saucepan, bring the gelatin and water to a simmer, whisking to combine. Once it reaches a simmer, shut off the heat and set aside.

In a stand mixer, mix the maple syrup, salt, and vanilla. Add the gelatin mixture and turn the mixer on low. Gradually increase the speed (so as not to splash it all out!) until the mixer reaches high.

Whip the marshmallow mixture until it forms soft peaks. It should have doubled in size during this time.

Butter a baking dish liberally, to keep the marshmallow mixture from sticking. Using a spatula, scrape the marshmallow mixture into the dish and smooth it out a bit. No need to be perfect, unless you're a perfectionist, in which case, good luck.

Refrigerate the homemade marshmallow mixture until it's just set, about an hour. At this point you can remove it from the refrigerator and slice it however you wish. Giving the cut marshmallows a toss in cornstarch, arrowroot powder, or icing sugar can keep them from sticking together.

4 tablespoons gelatin

⅔ cup cold water

1⅓ cups maple syrup or honey

Pinch of sea salt

½ teaspoon vanilla extract or the seeds from 1 vanilla pod

OUR DAILY SOURDOUGH BREAD

I've learned some major lessons in bread-making over the years. Much like painting, there truly is no end to the learning and experimenting that takes place. Forever a student, I had to go through a lot of trial and error to get this recipe just right. Here are a couple of lessons that drastically improved my bread-making abilities:

- Learn to make and keep a sourdough starter. Though I've tried a variety of flours to do so, bread flour has continually been my favorite because it produces a strong starter. The flavor from sourdough bread is unmatched.

- *Weigh* your ingredients instead of measuring them. This was suggested to me a few years ago and I've never looked back! Time after time, weighing produces a better bread, as different types of flours all aerate and measure differently. You can buy small digital scales for cheap, and they'll serve you well for years to come. **Makes 2 loaves**

200 grams sour-dough starter

630 grams water, divided

300 grams organic whole-grain flour (einkorn, rye, wheat, etc.)

700 grams organic bread flour

20 grams salt

In a stand mixer, combine the sourdough starter and 600 grams of the water.

Add the flours and mix again with the kneading hook, until the mixture forms a large ball.

Cover the mixing bowl with a wet tea towel and allow the flour to hydrate for 30 minutes to 2 hours.

Poke your fingers into the dough to create deep holes in it. In a small bowl, combine the salt and remaining 30 grams of water. Pour the water mixture into the holes.

Cover the dough again with the wet tea towel and let it sit for 30 minutes.

For a crispier crust, add a few cups of boiling water to a cast-iron skillet. Place the skillet on the bottom rack of a preheated oven, under the bread. This will keep the bread moist as it bakes. If you're using a dutch oven to bake the bread, the lid on top will create the same effect. Take the lid off for the last 10–12 minutes to get a deeply brown crust.

Scoop up one-quarter of the dough and flip it back on top of the remaining dough, using your fingertips to squish it in. Rotate the bowl and flip the next quarter of dough, flipping it onto the dough and squishing it in. Continue this flipping and folding until you've gone around the bowl three times. Cover with a wet tea towel and let it sit for 30 minutes.

Repeat the folding and resting process twice more.

Cover the bowl with plastic wrap and place it in the refrigerator for 12–24 hours. This step develops flavor, strengthens the structure of the bread, and also breaks down the hard-to-digest elements of the grain.

Remove the dough from the bowl carefully so as not to disturb all of those beautiful bubbles you've created, and separate it into two pieces. Shape each into a loaf and allow them to rest for an hour or two on a well-floured surface, covered with a wet tea towel, to come back to room temperature. Alternatively, it can be helpful to line small bowls with a heavily floured linen towel and allow the bread to rise in those. It keeps the dough growing up instead of out.

While the dough is rising, preheat the oven and a large baking stone, or two dutch ovens, to 475°F for an hour.

Carefully transfer the loaves, dusted with flour, to the preheated dish.

Bake for 40–50 minutes, until each loaf is deeply golden and hollow-sounding when tapped. Always err on the side of overbaking.

Remove the loaves from the oven and let them cool on a wire rack for a few hours before eating. I know it's hard to resist, but it's for the best.

SPROUTS

To get our fresh greens fix through the long, drawn-out winter months, I often opt for sprouting seeds. They will sprout in just a few days and can add a beautiful fresh taste and gentle crunch to almost any dish I'm serving. They're also loaded with nutrients to see us through until the first harvests of spring.

Add the seeds to a quart-size glass jar and fill the remainder of the jar with water.

Let the jar sit at room temperature for 12 hours.

Strain the seeds and rinse with fresh water in a mesh colander. Place the colander in a bowl (to catch any excess water that may drip out) and cover the bowl with a wet tea towel. Set aside.

Each morning and night, quickly grab the colander from the bowl and rinse it under fresh water. This will keep the seeds moist as they sprout and discourage the seeds from growing stagnant in the wet environment. After each rinsing, shake the colander to remove excess water, then place it back over the bowl and under the wet tea towel. Alternatively, if your seeds are super small, you can pour the contents of the colander into the bowl to keep them from getting stuck in the colander.

By the end of day three, you'll already have loads of sprouts! These can be eaten as is or left to grow for a few days more into even larger sprouts.

Serve over stir-fries, salads, and omelets, or just toss the sprouts with a nice dressing and enjoy them as is.

1 cup sprouting seeds, such as radish, lentil, wheat, broccoli, alfalfa, and pea (available online or through your health food store)

Filtered water

DUCK CONFIT

After we butcher our ducks in the late fall, duck confit—the classic French technique for preserving duck meat—is a treat that can be eaten on the darkest and coldest of winter days. It goes wonderfully with roasted potatoes or vegetables and a good chunk of that sourdough bread you just made. Go, you! **Serves 6**

¾ cup kosher salt

3 tablespoons dehydrated whole cane sugar (or sugar of choice)

6 duck legs and thighs, attached

1 teaspoon peppercorns

A few sprigs of fresh thyme

1 quart rendered duck fat, lard, or tallow

Combine the salt and sugar in a large bowl. Hold one duck leg and thigh at a time over the bowl and use your hands to sprinkle the salt mixture over the meat. Rub it in a bit to ensure the meat is evenly coated. Repeat with the remaining duck legs.

In another bowl, lay the salted legs down in a single layer. Sprinkle any remaining salt mixture over the top of them and then add the peppercorns and thyme. Use your fingertips to gently massage the salt in and around the legs once more. Cover with plastic wrap and stick the bowl in the refrigerator for 12–24 hours.

The next day, remove the legs from the salt and use a towel to wipe them clean and ensure they are dry.

Melt the fat in a heavy-bottomed stockpot. Add the duck legs in a single layer.

Gently simmer as low as possible for 1½–2 hours, until the meat is deeply golden and is just starting to pull away from the bone. The key is *low and slow.*

Once cooked, remove the duck legs from the pot and pack them into a glass container. Pour the melted fat from the stockpot over the top so that they're completely submerged in their own fat. Cover the

container and allow it to cool to room temperature. Transfer the container to the refrigerator for long-term storage.

With any luck, you'll remember it's there in a few months' time, though it can be eaten straightaway. Allow the container to come to room temperature before carefully removing one of the legs and thighs. Scrape off any remaining fat before quickly frying the leg up in a hot skillet and serving.

EINKORN GINGERBREAD COOKIES

I'm not a huge cookie person, but these cookies made from buttery einkorn flour and fresh ginger are quite wonderful in my book. I serve them plain because I enjoy their simplicity, but by all means, frost away. **Makes 2 dozen**

In a large bowl, sift together the flour, salt, and baking soda.

In another bowl, combine the butter, molasses, sugar, ginger, cinnamon, and eggs. Whisk well to completely combine.

Add the dry mixture to the wet mixture and fold with a spatula until just combined.

Remove the dough from the bowl and shape it into two discs. Wrap them in plastic wrap and refrigerate for 30 minutes.

Preheat the oven to 350°F. Using a heavily floured surface, roll the chilled dough out until it's ¼ inch thick. Cut the cookies to the desired shape, gather the remaining dough, and reroll it. Repeat the rolling and cutting process until all the dough has been utilized.

Bake the cookies in a 350°F oven on a baking sheet lined with parchment paper. Bake for 12–15 minutes, until the cookies are golden and just set. Remove the tray from the oven and allow the cookies to sit on the hot tray for an additional 10 minutes.

Remove the cookies to a wire rack and let them cool completely (if you can possibly bear to wait that long)!

6 cups all-purpose einkorn flour

1½ teaspoons salt

1 teaspoon baking soda

1 cup butter, melted

1 cup molasses

1 cup dehydrated whole cane sugar

2 tablespoons freshly ground ginger

2 teaspoons cinnamon

2 eggs

RAW OYSTERS WITH MIGNONETTE

Living in the Pacific Northwest, we have access to beautiful oysters that grow along the Washington coast. Each fall and winter, we find ourselves ordering from our family oyster company so that we can enjoy this luxury while it's at its best. Though there are countless ways to cook oysters—I'm sure many of them good—I've yet to find a way that I prefer more than just straight out of the shell. The subtle complexities of oysters should be appreciated and savored, just like many of our harvests. They taste like the seawater they grew in. **Serves 2-4**

⅓ cup raw apple cider vinegar

2 teaspoons dehydrated whole cane sugar

1 tablespoon minced shallot

½ teaspoon freshly ground black pepper

Pinch of sea salt

Pinch of red chili flakes

2 dozen oysters, shucked and on the half shell

In a small bowl, mix the vinegar, sugar, shallots, pepper, salt, and chili flakes. Whisk to combine.

Serve the oysters on the half shell with the mignonette sauce on the side. A small spoonful of the sauce with each oyster will do the job perfectly.

Winter in the Home

 I am excessively fond of a cottage; there is always so much comfort, so much elegance about them. —FROM SENSE AND SENSIBILITY *BY JANE AUSTEN*

As the cold season begins, the anticipation of Christmas is at hand and the house overflows with boughs of greenery. Large, sparkling trees fill our living rooms, and ornaments hang from the chandeliers and houseplants. It is a time to appreciate comfort and beautifully wrapped presents (or not so beautifully if you have my skills), and to add a bit of seasonal flair throughout the house. We often string garlands of popcorn or cranberries around the perimeter of the dining room, which adds to the homemade charm of the holidays.

This season is about homemade luxury, whether it's the smell of evergreen, extra mugs of hot chocolate, or spiced cookies. The smallest details, such as a pot of simmering mulled wine or a crackling fire in the fireplace, can instantly make the home feel inviting and comfortable. All of these details say *there is life here*, even if the world outside is deep in slumber.

On the flip side of the coin, after the holidays pass, we're faced with the second half of winter with no major holiday to look forward to. The presents have been opened, turkeys have been roasted and eaten, and trees have been dragged out to the compost pile. What we'll live with for the next few months is a post-party house in need of some TLC. For the homesteader, this is often the only time of year to focus on indoor projects. Before the seeds need to be sown, there is a window of opportunity to love on our spaces and thank them for serving our families well.

If your house is anything like mine with four farm kids, it takes a *beating*. Floors, furniture, walls, pillows, and bedding—all of it needs to be addressed. We live in every inch of our space, and that means every inch of our space needs a bit of refreshment. Around here, it's called "winter cleaning" because it's the only time of year I have nature's permission to stay indoors and tend to the details of the home. Which is exactly what I intend to do.

WINTER TEXTILES

Winter is often the time that I find myself washing, or replacing if necessary, all of my textiles. After the tree skirt has been packed away and the Christmas tablecloths stored in the closet for next year, I'm left with the everyday textiles I started the season with. Problem is, they're often a bit worse for the wear and tear. Will they last another year? How many more forts will my children create with them? I recently had a beautifully crocheted throw blanket fall apart in front of my eyes. It's a tough world out there.

Velvet. If I had to sum up my love for winter textiles in just one word, it would be *velvet*. Of course, the plaid always stays. And surely this wouldn't be the time to pack away the wool blankets. It's cold out there! But I can't help but appreciate the depth velvet adds to a space. Velvet curtains! Velvet accent tablecloths! Velvet throw pillows! I'll take them all.

Tweed. Stuart often wears tweed jackets to church, and I love the deeply textured and colored fabric. Two of our couches have been reupholstered in tweed out of pure love for its wearability, comfort, and vintage style. It's farmhouse meets old European style. Perfect.

Down. Most old houses are drafty and ours continues the tradition, primarily in the bedrooms. On the dark nights of winter, everyone's beds are layered with down blankets to keep the chill at bay. Extremely lightweight, they're perfect for little ones who scramble into bed and pull them quickly over their shivering bodies. I source my blankets from brands that hold to a no-live-pluck policy (IKEA, for example).

Toile. Most people are familiar with toile, even if they don't know what it's called. The French word, meaning "canvas," is a perfect translation for the beautiful image and stories that are created on the linen fabric. The drawings often depict old scenes from the farm, such as a milkmaid and her cows. I'm quite particular about my toile fabrics, often opting for vintage panels that are worn with time.

HAVE YOU EVER NOTICED . . .

That after a while, your throw pillows begin to look a little flat and stale? I've been known to throw all my pillows in a pile on the floor and let the kids jump around on them! It shifts the stuffing around a bit and wakes up the fabric so that they look freshened and perky when put back in place.

COTTAGE ELEMENTS FOR WINTER

One of the biggest gifts of the season is being able to shift our energy inward. Unlike spring and summer, when the outdoors demands almost all of my attention, winter gives me the luxury of being an intentional homemaker. Days are spent baking bread, schooling the children, and finishing off projects from the never-ending list. Though many may shudder at the idea of a projects list, I enjoy channeling my energy toward seeing something come to fruition.

Though it may sound challenging, one of the keys to creating intentional, beautiful spaces is to actually live in them. What do you see? What do you need from the space? Rooms that are lived in display messes and dirt, no doubt, but also incredible amounts of charm. Here at the cottage, I decorate with my family in mind first. I would encourage you to do the same. Allow your children to make forts with the blankets and pillows. Allow guests to put their feet up and forget to use a coaster. Allow the books you love to collect in large stacks on the table next to the sofa.

By cultivating an attitude of daily appreciation, we create an environment where memories are made. Remember, our rooms aren't for interior design shows. They're for our families and the people around us who we welcome in. Here's what I suggest:

Keep it fun. Don't be afraid to have stacks of board games, decks of cards, musical instruments, books, and favorite toys all around. Let the rooms reflect the people who live there. What good is it living in a perfectly beautiful home if creativity, personality, and a sense of fun is discouraged? Create reasons to celebrate. Shortest day of the year? Let's cook something special! Valentine's Day? Let's gather around the table and make cards for one another! Totally ordinary Wednesday? That's reason enough for champagne in my book. Don't underestimate the power of the ordinary.

Keep it mismatched. I used to buy things like teacups, plates, picture frames, and pillows in sets. But then I had kids. I learned that it's better to keep things mismatched in the first place. That way, I'm not crushed when a pair or trio is broken up. These days, I keep stacks of mismatched plates and bowls. Each of my couch pillows is a different design, and my coffee cup collection is quite eclectic. Even my socks are often mismatched (I should probably work on that).

Keep it genuinely rustic. Though rustic furniture is trending and you'll find all sorts of "French country" displays at all the major stores, hear me now: That's not my definition of rustic. I'd rather have an un-rustic table than a table that's pretending to be rustic. To counter the new-but-old style, I do one thing: I shop where there actually are old things—garage sales, thrift stores, antiques shops, and specialized online retailers. Bonus: These items are usually cheaper than their cheater counterparts. I think new, polished furniture certainly has its place, even in a rustic cottage, but if you're going to go "old," go authentic. Pair the polished with the genuinely rustic for contrast.

Keep it full of life. Plants and flowers are critical! If you tend to kill indoor plants (I've killed my fair share), opt instead for high-quality silks. Dried boxwoods or small faux olive trees are

DIY DISTRESSED TRIM

I do make an exception to my "keep it genuinely rustic" rule, and that's when it comes to distressing trim and wood. Using the same distressing method as found on page 117, hit up your molding. It adds the perfect amount of grunge to an otherwise styled and slightly polished room. The contrast is magic.

perfect additions. Take a step back and ask yourself, Where's the life in this space? That often helps to pinpoint what's missing.

Learn the art of the vignette. I learned the art of the vignette by making front-of-store displays. In reference to interior design, a vignette is a "picture" created by grouping a few objects together. Try this: Hold your hands out about 6 inches in front of you and use your fingers to create a vertical box. Close one of your eyes and peer through the box. What do you see?

Here are some features I like in my vignettes:

- **Light.** Lamps, sconces, chandeliers, or candles keep the area full of life.

- **Greenery.** Plants, flowers, even faux succulents or twigs will do. Again, greenery points to freshness and to life.

- **Texture.** A metallic mirror frame, for example, could be paired next to a knobby vintage tablecloth. Old wood can be paired with sleek new lamps. Mixing it up keeps it interesting!

- **Height.** Again, mix it up. Incorporate tall vases with short picture frames, or large pieces of art on the wall with stacks of books on the floor.

- **The home's theme.** I like to play with vintage books on farming, old ceramic flower pots, maps of the English countryside, old wooden spools, bust statues, galvanized pots, dried flowers, copper planters, wooden baskets, vintage linens, stacks of wood, and even rusty metal pans. All of this fits with our home's theme. As you figure out the theme of your home, be consistent as you bring it from room to room.

Creating the perfect vignette is a domestic art form. I think of vignettes as the pictures I get to paint around my home. I never tire of "painting" and often find myself shifting furniture around so I can do just that.

"BLESS THE HOUSE"

Years ago, my husband was tipped off to an idea that some people call "bless the house," and it's a habit we quickly adopted and our children now know well. At various times of the day, we will all gather to bless the house, which means that everyone pitches in to pick up the entire house as quickly as possible. The music is turned up loud. Our older daughter, Georgia, is often in charge of putting away dishes, books, and art supplies while the boys, Owen and Will, gather up the scattered toys and dirty laundry. Someone will wipe the dining table, someone will sweep up the floor, and someone else will put fresh oils in the diffuser. Little Juliette just toddles around from room to room, distracting the rest of us. I

usually find myself elbow deep in soapy water, scrubbing up the last of the dishes, wiping off countertops, lighting a candle, and gathering up all of the throw blankets that have found their way to the floor *again*.

Though it's never perfect, this ten-minute sprint keeps the house fresh. We're sometimes called to open our doors for hospitality at a moment's notice. Blessing the house enables us to maintain a positive environment for everyone who's in it.

CLEANING THE HOME NATURALLY

It'd be fair to say that one of my first skills as a newlywed was cleaning the home naturally. Long before I'd learned to cook a proper omelet, I had already ditched any and all commercial cleaners in lieu of homemade ones. On a lunch break at the flower shop, I flipped through an old magazine and came across an article that tipped me off to the chemicals that the majority of cleaners contained. That article was one of my very first steps toward a more holistic approach to my home, my food, and eventually, my farm.

Though money no longer dictates being able to purchase natural cleaners (as it did when we were first married), I still find joy in making my own. I employ a lot of essential oils in my homemade cleaners because they're pure, potent, and powerful. Many essential oils are naturally antimicrobial, antibacterial, and antifungal. Plus, they boost the immune system and can be utilized in multiple ways, making them a complete workhorse on the farm. When the winter blues hit, I know it's time to deep-clean spaces with oils. The aromatherapy, coupled with the therapeutic nature of cleaning, can work wonders on gloomy days.

Here are a few of my favorite concoctions for cleaning. I include my favorite oils, but by all means, substitute the ones you like! Just make sure they're high quality.

GLASS CLEANER

2 cups distilled water

½ cup vinegar

½ cup rubbing alcohol (or vodka)

15 drops wild orange essential oil

Combine all the ingredients in a squirt bottle and shake well. Spray on mirrors and windows and wipe clean.

GUNK REMOVER

Lemon essential oil

Lemon oil has incredible gunk-removing abilities! For residues such as those from stickers, simply add a bit of lemon oil to them, let sit for a minute, and scrub it off.

TOILET AND SINK SCRUB

1 cup washing soda (available in the cleaning aisle of your local grocery store)

2 cups baking soda

10 drops melaleuca (tea tree) oil

10 drops lemon essential oil

White vinegar, for rinsing

Mix the washing soda, baking soda, and oils in a container. Add a small amount to the sink or toilet and scrub. Let the mixture sit for 5–10 minutes before rinsing it down with vinegar.

FLOOR CLEANER

1 gallon hot water

2 tablespoons natural dish soap

1 cup white vinegar

10 drops eucalyptus essential oil

10 drops lemon essential oil

Mix all of the ingredients in a large bucket and use for mopping or scrubbing as needed.

CARPET FRESHENER

3 cups baking soda

30 drops lemon, wild orange, or peppermint oil

Combine the ingredients in a container and let it sit overnight (or make ahead and just keep a stash on hand!). The next day, shake the mixture over your carpet and let it sit again overnight. Vacuum up the following day.

ALL-PURPOSE CLEANER

2 cups distilled water

2 cups white vinegar

1 teaspoon natural dish soap

5 drops rosemary oil

5 drops lavender oil

5 drops lemon oil

Combine all of the ingredients in a squirt bottle. Use it on all your surfaces for general cleaning.

"LIGHT THE CANDLE"

The days of an entrepreneurial, homeschooling farm family are long. I'm up at 4:00 a.m., which is when I can sneak downstairs to our cozy office to answer emails, write a few words, and make goals for the day, all while I sip my first cup of home-roasted coffee. During the summer, I'll ditch office work and trudge out into the garden as the sun first appears.

During the week, our mornings are filled with homeschooling (or "farmschooling" as I like to call it). Stuart and I tag team by covering different subjects and projects. Some days the focus is on academics as we practice math equations, and other times it's on observing nature as we watch a ewe give birth. Little mouths ask questions about all kinds of subjects, whether it's music, art, language, farm animals, or the weather. They certainly never stop inquiring. My son William asked me recently why I'm awake when he goes to bed and awake when he rises. "Why don't mommies sleep at night?" Good question, my love.

After farmschool comes farm work. Everyone pitches in to clean coops, scrape stalls, pick up trash, move animals, or gather eggs. In the winter, the work centers around keeping the animals comfortable with extra straw bedding and full water tanks. We begin to lamb and farrow in the cold days of January, so we're often on baby watch as well. There's hardly anything more fun than spending a cold day watching a ewe or sow give birth to new farm life. It serves as a promise of what's to come in the spring—*a new beginning!*

The only thing that draws us back indoors is the promise of a hot meal on the supper table. Home-harvested meat and winter-stored vegetables are always at the top of the list, as they warm the belly like a comforting hug. A glass of wine doesn't hurt either.

Throughout the day, there might be bickering among the children (and adults), so many dirty dishes it'll make your head spin, and discouraging setbacks on the farm. That's part of life. But at the end of it all, when the last dish is washed, the counters are wiped clean, and toys, clothes, shoes, and random items are picked up off the kitchen floor and put away, I have a ritual.

A single candle sits in an old whiskey bottle on my butcher-block counter. I light it when the storm of the day has passed. I light it when it's perfectly acceptable to put on my pajamas and curl up on the couch with a book. I light it when, even if imperfect, I can shut the house down for the day and submit to the calm darkness of the night and season. A friend of mine has the same habit, and we often send each other pictures of this "light the candle" time. A time of rest, reflection, and restoration.

It all begins again tomorrow.

THE ART OF REST

Curled up by the fireplace is usually where I find him. The popping sound from the burning cherrywood and cedar is a dead giveaway. The sound is often accompanied by the smell of espresso. All that's left is to listen for the sound of silence, or rather, the sound of pages being turned. For Stu, this is the sound of rest.

My children, on the other hand, usually recharge by *actually* sleeping, as they're still learning the art of fire building, coffee drinking, and reading. Give 'em a few years, they'll be fine. For now, they fill their time with bug encyclopedias and a box of crayons.

I have a variety of forms of rest, though working in the garden and cooking goodies in the kitchen are my favorites. Knitting, reading, and flipping through seed catalogs can also keep me busy for hours on these dark days. I'm often found with tea in hand, doodling out the gardens for the coming spring or picking out the perfect shade of foxglove to be planted.

In a culture that scrambles to and fro, constantly seeking the next thrill and glorifying the "busyness" of life, it takes practice to rest. To still the mind, silence the outside world, and recharge sometimes feels nearly impossible. For our family, rest begins by only taking on commitments and obligations that are fitting for us at this stage of life.

It takes practice and intention to create value in rest. As the saying goes, "Don't live for the next vacation; create a life you don't have to take a vacation from" (or something like that). Pockets of rest, found by the fireplace, in front of the art easel, or in the kitchen, quiet the noise of life.

Cultivate silence, restoration, and rest.

REALITY CHECK

Just because we're cultivating rest doesn't mean life is all calm and collected. What it does mean is that as the mess comes, which it will, we're in a better place mentally to handle the madness. Enter the winter farm closet.

Some farms have mudrooms. What a brilliant invention . . . that unfortunately doesn't exist in our world. Instead, we have a small closet that is host to almost every boot, jacket, glove, and pair of coveralls we own. When there are six people who have to get out the door for farm chores in the morning, can you imagine the chaos as gloves fly and scarves are tossed?

THE COLORS OF WINTER

In the winter, we like to bring in large bunches of greenery to "deck the halls." Ruby red ornaments dangle from tree branches, and gold lights flicker from the foliage. Even the dishes served this time of year boast "roasted" shades of brown, cream, and green. We pour dark red wine into glasses and slice purple beets and golden onions. It is a feast for the eyes!

I find that rich jewel tones and warm colors bring me the most comfort. An all-white room, for example, doesn't make me feel like tucking in. Give me shades of the Scottish countryside! Give me dark tweed! Give me burgundy and emerald and champagne (the color, not the drink . . . actually, I think I'll take the drink as well)! The cottage should feel like a warm, comfortable, and eclectic visual hug. There's no greater vehicle for establishing that than with color.

ACCENT WALLS

Aesthetically speaking, accent walls are rarely a good idea. They tend to visually break the flow of a space. Instead, you can incorporate a favorite bold color with your furniture, throw pillows, or art.

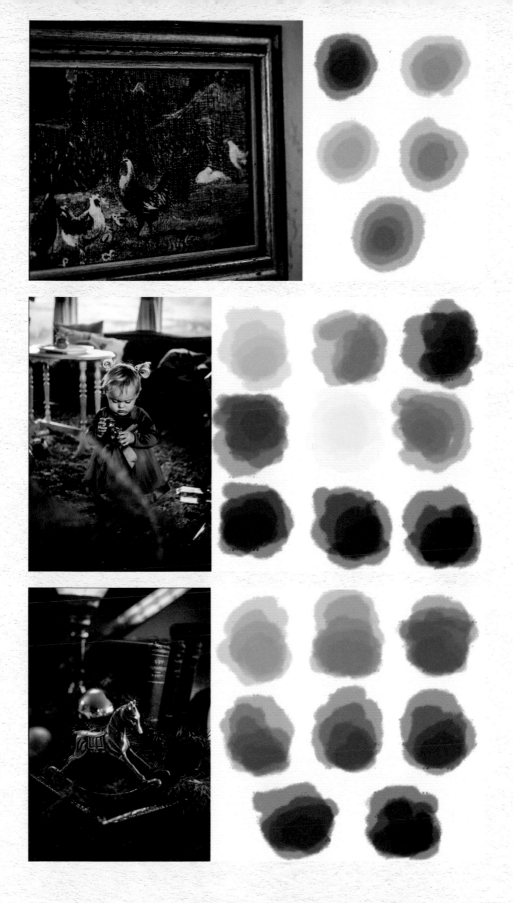

Winter Celebrations

I believe that a godly home is a foretaste of heaven. Our homes,
imperfect as they are, must be a haven from the chaos outside.
They should be a reflection of our eternal home, where troubled
souls find peace, weary hearts find rest, hungry bodies find
refreshment, lonely pilgrims find communion, and wounded
spirits find compassion. —JANI ORTLUND

While I was backpacking through Europe, I remember a particularly low point. We'd missed a few trains, finally arriving at our hotel late into the night, weary and fatigued. We were promptly encouraged to head to the restaurant up the road a little ways to drink and eat our worries away. We obliged.

The road to the restaurant was dark. The Italian countryside had consumed the path and branches arched over, all but blocking out the night sky. Completely unsure of our chosen route (and life choices at this point), we kept driving on even though we were tired. I'll never forget looking up from the bleak road and seeing the light from the restaurant on the hillside. Nestled in among the trees, I still couldn't make out the actual building. Rather, I saw the glow

from a few glass windows, pouring out onto the road. For a traveler, weak in spirit, there was nothing more comforting. That light said, "Come. Eat. Drink. Be filled. Let us care for you." And I let them.

As I open the door and shuffle in guests to our home, my hope is always that they'll be restored, that even something as small as a meal, conversation and laughter, and a glass of port will be enough to "fill their cups" for the coming days. Le Chalet is nestled down at the bottom of a gravel road. You must drive around a few bends of cherry trees before the light from the cottage can be seen. There are no streetlights or sidewalks on the farm. The light from the cottage kitchen is the first one seen from the driveway.

After pulling up, guests can then easily peer into the glass French doors that open from the courtyard into the dining room, most likely witnessing a set table with candles burning and the wine opened. Like that restaurant on the hill in Italy, our cottage offers the same to our guests. Arriving in the darkness of a winter night, our guests follow the warm lights into the cottage. Upon their arrival, we say, "Come. Eat. Drink. Be filled. Let us care for you."

I've mentioned that my mom taught me how to set the stage for celebrating with company. Here are the essentials I return to again and again for setting the winter table:

Rich foods. There is most certainly a time for clean soups and entree salads, but in my humble opinion, it is not winter. Rather, the table should be filled with artisan cheeses, roasted meats

and vegetables, flavorful wines, succulent desserts, whole-grain breads, and plenty of butter. I want guests to feel as if they've been given a warm embrace, which is exactly what rich foods accomplish.

Comfort. A secondhand, casual tablecloth, wearing the stains from all the meals it's served over the decades, makes guests feel instantly comfortable. This isn't the type of table to exclude little ones or even messy adults from enjoying the food on their plates. Likewise, the warm glow of candlelight also makes guests feel calm and cozy as it flickers across the table.

Family style. More often than not, this is the way we serve guests. The finished dishes are displayed on a variety of plates and platters before being brought out to the table. Large serving spoons are tucked into each dish before it's passed around from hand to hand, each guest serving himself. Not only does this keep the table casual, but it automatically makes guests feel comfortable. After all, they get to choose what and how much ends up on their plate. It doesn't hurt that the dishes are within arm's reach for easy second servings either.

Food with stories. The table may be simple, yet serving up food that we've labored to produce over the past year runs incredibly deep. Behind every vegetable is years of knowledge put to use as we combat the dry, hot summers. The meat is a

reflection of more than a decade setting the foundation for our own breeding livestock, raising them on pasture and then harvesting them in the most resourceful, respectful way. The fruits have been picked, preserved, and put away for such a night as this. Even the small cups that litter the table are filled with milk that is hand-squeezed each morning, by yours truly and my faithful companion, from a cow with a name. Each element of the table has a story.

After the obvious celebration of winter has passed, we're left with dozens of ordinary days. A cold, dreary, perhaps snow-filled Monday is just as much a part of winter as the holidays, and truth be told, can be just as magical. There is no day of the week that doesn't benefit from sharing the table. These short, dark days and how we spend them begin to define our season. To embrace the simplicity of winter, with its rich solitude and comfortable provisions, is a beautiful start to defining our everyday ordinary.

Another day of gratitude for warm bodies, full bellies, delicious food and drink, and safety from the elements that sweep down from the mountains into our little valley. A refuge in the storm, for our family and guests alike.

This is our winter table.

AFTERWORD

The ornament of a house is the friends who frequent it.
—RALPH WALDO EMERSON

Truth be told, I was a bit hesitant to open up our home for this book. As a blogger, I've made my living opening up pieces of my life for people to connect with, but never in such a raw and unfiltered sense. Holding to the truth that some things are better left to the imagination, I haven't shown you my dirty laundry or muddy bathroom. As an artist, I also felt discomfort in preserving our farm in photographs that capture a moment in time. You see, our home and garden are constantly morphing (you may have noticed the same pieces of furniture in two or more different spots throughout the house as the seasons go on). We're only two years into the renovation of Le Chalet, and there is much more to come—bedroom and bathroom remodels, barns, new pastures, a mother-in-law cottage, a greenhouse, market gardens, and more. So why would I display an unfinished piece of my art? Because seasons on the farm are just that.

Life on the farm is never clean and rarely finished. Gardens require work each year, cows require milking each morning, and apples require picking each fall. The seasons bring with them a steady routine, though they're always slightly unique. The seasonal home is no different. And so, imperfect and incomplete as it may be, our doors are open for fellowship. On these few acres, there is a

steady stream of work and food flowing through daily. Even if there are walls to be painted and ducks to move to new pasture, the work and food carry on. It is a canvas that shifts with seasonal shadows, morning sunrises, and new animals, making it the artist's ultimate challenge and joy.

I charge forward at Le Chalet knowing there is more bread to bake, beets to plant, espressos to sip, and stories to read. It's work I'll never tire of. My prayer is that I've inspired you to cultivate beauty wherever you are, with whatever you've got.

May the work in our homes, and our hearts, be beautiful.

ACKNOWLEDGMENTS

I'm ever amazed at the work that goes into producing something worth reading. Without a team behind a project like this, it would surely fail to "sing." I'm ever thankful for the support of my team who has helped me, once again, produce something truly beautiful.

To editor Holly Rubino, who can take a bird's-eye view of a project and whip it into shape! Thank you, Holly, for pushing me to think deeper and write better.

To production editor Meredith Dias and copyeditor Elissa Curcio, for their incredibly detail-oriented minds. Thank you for polishing this book until it sparkled! Feel free to edit these acknowledgments as well. . . .

To the entire Lyons Press team for their creativity and continual belief in our projects, including designer Diana Nuhn and layout artist Melissa Evarts.

To Sally, my literary agent, who continues to be a cheerleader in my corner. None of this would have started without you, and we're blessed to be a part of the Lisa Ekus Group.

To my parents, who've taught me how to have an open home and open table.

To Janine, my design mentor, who's taught me more than she realizes.

To my beautiful family, who are the reason I create.

To God be the glory.

ABOUT THE AUTHOR

Shaye Elliott is the founder of the blog *The Elliott Homestead*, which she began in 2010 when her farm was but a dream. She and her husband, Stuart, are now developing their own little farm in the Pacific Northwest with their quiver of children, Georgia, Owen, William, and Juliette. Shaye spends her days writing, gardening, child and chicken wrangling, cow milking, pig wrestling, wine sipping, and dreaming. She is the author of *From Scratch*, *Family Table*, and *Welcome to the Farm*. She lives in Malaga, Washington.